St. Paul

St. Paul

THE APOSTLE WE LOVE TO HATE

KAREN ARMSTRONG

ICONS SERIES

amazonpublishing

Published by Amazon Publishing, New York

www.apub.com

Amazon, the Amazon logo and Amazon Publishing are trademarks of
Amazon.com, Inc. or its affiliates.

ISBN-10: 1477828338
ISBN-13: 9781477828335

Cover design by Emily Weigel, Faceout Studio
Cover illustration by Antar Dayal

For Jenny Wayman

Contents

St. Paul

Introduction

WHILE JERUSALEM WAS celebrating Passover c. 30 CE, Pontius Pilate, Roman governor of Judea, ordered the crucifixion of a peasant from the tiny hamlet of Nazareth in Galilee. Passover was nearly always an explosive time in the Holy City, where Roman rule was bitterly resented. Pilate and Caiaphas, the high priest, had probably agreed to deal promptly with any potential troublemaker, so they would certainly have taken careful note of Jesus of Nazareth's provocative entrance into the city a week earlier, riding on a donkey as Zechariah had prophesied and acknowledging the homage of the enthusiastic crowd, who shouted: "Liberate us, Son of David!" Was he claiming to be the longed-for Messiah, a descendant of the great King David who would free Israel from foreign bondage? As if that were not enough, Jesus had immediately charged into the temple and overturned the money changers' tables, accusing them of making this sacred place a den of thieves. When he was nailed to his cross, "an inscription was placed over his head, citing the charge against him: 'This is Jesus, the king of the Jews.'"[1]

Jesus had been born during the reign of the emperor Augustus (r. 31 BCE–14 CE), who had brought peace to a war-weary world by defeating rival Roman warlords and declaring himself sole ruler of the Roman Empire. The ensuing peace seemed little short of miraculous, and throughout his far-flung domains, Augustus was hailed as "son of God" and "savior." But the Pax Romana was enforced pitilessly by an army that was the most efficient killing machine the world had yet seen; the slightest resistance met with wholesale slaughter. Crucifixion, an instrument of state terror inflicted usually on slaves, violent criminals, and insurgents, was a powerful deterrent. The public display of the flayed victim, his broken body hanging at a crossroads or in a theater and, all too often, left as food for birds of prey and wild beasts, demonstrated the merciless power of Rome.[2] Some thirty years before Jesus's death, after crushing the revolts that had broken out after the death of King Herod the Great, the Syrian governor P. Quinctilius Varus had crucified two thousand rebels at once outside the walls of Jerusalem.[3] Forty years after Jesus's death, in the last days of the Roman siege of Jerusalem (70 CE), starving deserters trying to flee the doomed city, averaging about five hundred a day, were scourged, tortured, and crucified. The Jewish historian Josephus, an eyewitness, recorded the horrifying spectacle: "The soldiers out of rage and hatred amused themselves by nailing their prisoners in different postures; and so great was their number, that space could not be found for the crosses nor crosses for the bodies."[4]

One of the most terrible things about crucifixion was that the victim was denied a decent burial, a disgrace that was insupportable in the ancient world in a way that is difficult for modern people to appreciate. The victim was usually left alive to be torn apart by carrion crows. In Judea, if the soldiers were persuaded to observe the Jewish law decreeing that a body be buried immediately after its demise, they might lay it in a shallow grave where it would soon be devoured by the wild scavenger dogs that prowled hungrily below the dying man. But from a very early date, Jesus's followers were convinced that Jesus had been buried in a respectable tomb, and, later, the authors of the four gospels developed an elaborate story to explain how his disciples had persuaded the Roman authorities to permit this.[5] This was a crucial element in the earliest Christian tradition.[6]

Jesus's atrocious death would be central to the religious and political vision of Saul of Tarsus, the first extant Christian author. Paul was his Roman name. In the West, we have deliberately excluded religion from political life and regard faith as an essentially private activity. But this is a modern development, dating only to the eighteenth century, and would have been incomprehensible to both Jesus and Paul. Jesus's demonstration in the temple was not, as is often assumed, a plea for a more spiritual form of worship. As he rampaged through the money changers' stalls, he quoted the Hebrew prophets who had harsh words for those who were punctilious in their devotions but ignored the plight of the poor, the vulnerable, and the oppressed. For nearly five hundred years, Judea had been ruled by one empire after another, and the temple, the holiest place in the Jewish world, had become an instrument of imperial control. Since 63 BCE, the Romans had ruled Judea in conjunction with the priestly aristocracy, who collected the tribute extorted in kind from the populace and stored it in the temple precincts. Over the years, this collaboration had brought the institution into such disrepute that peasants were refusing to pay the temple tithe.[7] At Qumran, beside the Dead Sea, Jewish sectarians were so disgusted with this corruption of their most sacred institutions that they had withdrawn from mainstream society, convinced that God would soon destroy the temple and replace it with a purified shrine not made by human hands. So Jesus was not the only person to regard the temple as a "den of thieves," and his violent demonstration, which probably cost him his life, would have been understood by the authorities as a threat to the political order.

Galilee, the scene of Jesus's mission in the north of what is now the state of Israel, was home to a society traumatized by imperial violence. Nazareth was only a few miles from the town of

Sepphoris, which the Roman legions had razed to the ground during the uprisings after Herod's death. Herod Antipas, the sixth son of Herod the Great, governed the region as the client of Rome and had financed his extensive building program by imposing heavy taxes on his subjects, laying claim to crops, livestock, and labor and expropriating between 50 to 66 percent of the peasants' produce. Failure to pay the required tax was punished by foreclosure and confiscation of land, which swelled the estates of the Herodian aristocracy, as well as those of the bankers and bureaucrats who flocked into the region to make their fortunes.[8] When they lost land that had been in their family for generations, the more fortunate peasants worked on it as serfs; others were forced into banditry or menial labor. This could have happened to Jesus's father, Joseph the carpenter.

In about 28 CE, huge crowds had flocked from Judea, Jerusalem, and the surrounding countryside to listen to the fiery preaching of John the Baptist beside the River Jordan. Clad in rough camel's hair that recalled the garb of the prophet Elijah, John had urged them to undergo baptism as a token of repentance to hasten the coming of the Kingdom that God would establish to displace the wicked rulers of this age. This was no purely spiritual message. When members of the priestly aristocracy and their retainers presented themselves for baptism, John denounced them as a "viper's brood"; they would not be saved on the Day of Judgment simply because they were descendants of Abraham.[9] In Israel, ritual immersion had long signified not only a moral purification but also a social commitment to justice. "Your hands are covered with blood," the prophet Isaiah had told the ruling class of Jerusalem in the eighth century BCE. "Wash, make yourselves clean. Take your wrongdoing out of my sight. Learn to do good, search for justice, help the oppressed, be just to the orphan, and plead for the widow."[10] The sectarians at Qumran performed frequent ablutions, both as a rite of purification and as a political commitment "to observe justice to men" and "to hate the unjust and fight the battle of the righteous ones."[11] But John offered baptism not merely to an elite group but also to the common people. When these impoverished, indebted folk asked him what they should do, he told them to share what little they had with those who were even worse off — an ethic that would become central to Jesus's movement: "Whoever has two shirts must share with him who has none, and whoever has food must do the same."[12]

Jesus was among the people baptized by John; when he emerged from the water, it was said that the Holy Spirit descended upon him and a heavenly voice proclaimed: "You are my beloved Son in whom I delight."[13] After their baptism, all Jesus's followers would later cry aloud that they too had become children of God and members of a community where everybody lived as equals. The Spirit would be crucial to this early movement; it was not a separate divine being, of course, but a term used by Jews to denote the presence and power of God in human life. When John was arrested by Antipas c. 29 CE, Jesus began his own mission in Galilee, "armed with the power of the Spirit."[14] Crowds thronged around him, just as they had come to John, to hear his startling message: "The Kingdom of God has already arrived."[15] Its coming was not scheduled in a remote future; the Spirit, the active presence of God, was evident *now* in Jesus's miracles of healing. Everywhere he looked, he saw people pushed to the limit, abused, and crushed. "He felt sorry for them because they were harassed [*eskulemenoi*] and dejected [*errimmenoi*], like sheep without a shepherd."[16] The Greek verbs chosen by the evangelist had political as well as emotional connotations of being "beaten down" by imperial predation.[17] They were hungry, physically sick, psychologically disturbed, and probably suffering from the effects of the hard labor, poor sanitation, overcrowding, indebtedness, and acute anxiety endured by the masses in any premodern agrarian economy.[18] In Jesus's parables, we see a society in which rich and poor are separated by an impassable gulf; where people are desperate for loans, heavily indebted, and preyed upon by unscrupulous landlords; and where the dispossessed are forced to hire themselves out as day laborers.[19]

It is almost impossible to construct an accurate picture of the historical Jesus. Paul, writing twenty years after Jesus's death, is the earliest extant Christian writer, but he tells us next to nothing about Jesus's earthly life. The four canonical gospels were written much later — Mark in the late 60s, Matthew and Luke in the 80s and 90s, and John c. 100, all four deeply affected by the Jewish War (66–73 CE) that resulted in the destruction of Jerusalem and its temple. Living in one of the most violent periods of Jewish history, so terrible that it seemed like the End of Days, the evangelists struggled to make sense of the hideous death toll, the massive devastation, and the widespread suffering and bereavement. As they did so, they seem to have introduced a fiery, apocalyptic element into their gospels that may not have been present in Jesus's original teaching. Scholars have noted that Matthew and Luke both based their accounts not only on Mark's narrative but also on another text that has not survived, which they quoted almost verbatim. Scholars call this lost gospel "Q," from the German *quelle* ("source"). We do not know exactly when it was written, but because it does not refer at all to the Jewish War, it was probably put together in Galilee sometime before 66 and may even have been committed to writing as early as the 50s, at the same time Paul was dictating his own letters to the scribe. Unlike the canonical gospels, Q did not tell the story of Jesus's life but was simply a collection of his sayings. In Q, therefore, we have a source that may bring us closer to what Jesus told the troubled people of Galilee.

At the heart of this proto-gospel is the Kingdom of God.[20] This was not a fiery apocalypse descending from on high but essentially a revolution in community relations. If people set up an alternative society that approximated more closely to the principles of God recorded in Jewish law, they could hasten the moment when God intervened to change the human condition. In the Kingdom, God would be sole ruler, so there would be no Caesar, no procurator, and no Herod. To make the Kingdom a reality in the desperate conditions in which they lived, people must behave *as if* the Kingdom had already come.[21] Unlike the state of affairs in Herodian Galilee, the benefits of God's Kingdom were not confined to a privileged elite, because the Kingdom was open to everybody, especially the "destitute" and the "beggar" (*ptochos*) whom the current regime had failed.[22] You should not invite only your rich neighbors to a feast, Jesus told his host at a dinner. "No, when you have a party, invite the poor, the crippled, the blind, and the lame." Invitations must be delivered "in the streets and alleys of the town" and "the open roads and hedgerows."[23] It was a politically explosive message: In the Kingdom the first would be last and the last first.[24]

In this Kingdom, Jesus taught, men and women must love even their enemies, giving them practical and moral support. Instead of taking cruel reprisals for injury, as the Romans did, they must live according to the Golden Rule: "To the man who slaps you on one cheek, present the other cheek too; to the man who takes your cloak from you, do not refuse your tunic. Give to everyone who asks you, and do not ask for your property back from the man who robs you. Treat others as you would like them to treat you."[25] The Lord's Prayer is the prayer of the Kingdom, uttered by people who could only hope to have enough food for one day at a time, who were terrified of falling into debt and being hauled to the tribunal that would confiscate their small holdings:

> *Father — Holy be Your Name! — may your empire come!*
> *Give us each day our daily bread;*
> *And forgive us our debts, for we also have forgiven our*
>   *debtors.*
> *And lead us not into trial.*[26]

There was nothing novel in Jesus's teaching. The ancient laws of Israel had urged exactly this kind of self-help and mutual aid. According to what may be the earliest strands of the Torah (the Law of Moses), instead of being appropriated by an aristocracy, land should remain in the possession of the extended family; interest-free loans to needy Israelites were obligatory; contract servitude was restricted; and special provision was made for the socially vulnerable — orphans, widows, and foreigners.[27] At the end of every seven years, all debts must be remitted and slaves set free. Wealthy Israelites must be openhanded with the poor and give them enough for their needs.[28]

Jesus dispatched his disciples — fishermen, despised tax collectors, and farmers — to implement this program in the Galilean villages. It was in effect a practical declaration of independence. His followers need not become serfs, laboring for the enrichment of others; they could simply take themselves out of the system and create an alternative economy, surviving by sharing whatever they had.[29] The American scholar John Dominic Crossan believes that in Jesus's instructions to these missionaries, we find the kernel of the early Jesus movement. When they arrived in a village, Jesus told them, they must knock on a door and wish the householder peace; if he was kind enough to admit them, they must stay in that house, working with their hosts and "sharing their food and drink: for the worker deserves his pay... When you enter a town and you are made welcome, eat the food provided for you, heal the sick there, and say: 'The Kingdom of God has come upon you.'"[30] The Kingdom became present whenever somebody had the compassion to admit a needy stranger to his home, when that stranger received food from another and then offered something in return. Peasants, Crossan explains, had two overriding anxieties: "Shall I eat today?" and "Shall I become ill and fall into debt?" In Jesus's system, if one person had food then everybody could eat, and there would always be somebody to care for the sick. This interdependence and mutual sharing was both a Way of Salvation and a Way of Survival.[31]

This was not simply a social program masquerading as religion; premodern men and women had no concept of the secular as we know it. All the great spiritual traditions have insisted that what holds us back from enlightenment is selfishness and egotism; they have also said that a practical concern for everybody (not simply those who belong to your own class or those you find congenial) was the test of true spirituality. By making the heroic effort to share their meager resources, withhold their anger and desire for vengeance, and minister to others even when they were enfeebled themselves, Jesus's and, later, Paul's followers were systematically dethroning themselves from the center of their world and putting another there. They were thus achieving the selfless state of mind that others have sought in yoga, the aim of which is to extract the "I" from our thinking and behavior — the self-obsession that limits our humanity and holds us back from the transcendence known variously as Brahman, Dao, Nirvana, or God.

But Jesus knew that some people would hate this program and even regard it as seditious. He warned his disciples that it would set people against one another and split families.[32] In Roman Palestine, anyone who followed him had to be prepared for the ordeal of the cross.[33] His teachings were difficult: Not everybody wanted to love his enemies, turn his back on his family, if necessary, and leave the dead to bury the dead.[34] The later portions of Q show that Jesus's envoys encountered opposition and rejection, especially from those who feared or were reliant upon the Herodian system.[35] When Jesus arrived in Jerusalem to proclaim the Kingdom and denounced the extortion and injustice of the priestly aristocracy, he was executed as a dissident.

The crucifixion could have spelled the end of the Jesus movement. But some members of Jesus's inner circle, who seem to have fled Jerusalem and returned to Galilee after his arrest, had startling visions in which they saw his broken, bleeding body raised to new life, standing, vindicated, at the right hand of God's throne in the highest place in Heaven. This, they concluded, meant that God had designated Jesus as the *Messiah*, the "anointed" descendant of King David who would establish God's Kingdom and inaugurate a reign of justice. The first to see the risen Jesus was Simon, also called Peter or Cephas ("Rock"); next Jesus appeared to a group of disciples known henceforth as the Twelve and then to a crowd of more than five hundred of his followers; finally he appeared to his brother James.[36] An outpouring of the Spirit accompanied these extraordinary visions, which empowered these frightened men to go public, uttering inspired prophecy and performing miracles of healing, convinced that this was the new age predicted by the prophet Joel:

> *I will pour out my spirit on all mankind*
> *Your sons and daughters shall prophesy*
> *Your old men shall dream dreams,*
> *And your young men see visions.*
> *Even on the slaves, men and women,*
> *I will pour out my spirit in those days.*[37]

In the past, prophets had usually been aristocrats attached to the royal court, but now the Spirit was inspiring humble members of society — fishermen, carpenters, artisans, and peasants — to inform their fellow Israelites that Jesus, the Messiah, would soon return to inaugurate God's Kingdom. His resurrection was no mythical event of the distant past; Jesus's exaltation had been witnessed by hundreds of people who were still very much alive and well.

In ancient times, the Hebrew term *messhiah* had applied to anyone — a king, priest, or prophet — who had been doused with oil in a ceremony that appointed him to a divinely ordained task. But when Israel came under imperial rule, the title began to acquire a wholly new significance, as people looked forward to a different kind of king, a son of David endowed with righteousness and understanding, who would restore Israel's lost dignity. According to the Psalms of Solomon, the Anointed One would liberate the Jewish people, expose corrupt officials, drive all foreign sinners out of the land, and reign in Jerusalem, which would once again become a holy city, attracting nations "from the ends of the earth."[38] This text was written in Jerusalem during the first century BCE but had been translated into Greek and was widely read in the diaspora, where Jews living under Roman occupation also looked forward to the coming of the Messiah (*Christos* in Greek). This was, of course, potentially seditious; it would be even more subversive if the man revered as the Christ had been executed by a Roman governor.

Q mentions neither Jesus's death nor his resurrection; perhaps the Q community could not bear to think about his crucifixion and either did not know about the resurrection appearances or disapproved of them. They continued their mission but seem to have disappeared during the mayhem of the Jewish War. For the Twelve, however, the death of Jesus was not something to be glossed over, because it had saving power. In Judaism, a martyr was said to have died for the "sins" of Israel. This did not mean the personal faults of individual Israelites but the failure of the people as a whole to observe the divine commandments and carry out their social responsibilities — failings that God had punished with political catastrophe. His readiness to die for these principles made the martyr a role model. Jesus's martyrdom, therefore, was a spur to action and would inspire continued effort to hasten the Kingdom.

So after their life-changing visions, the Twelve left Galilee and returned to Jerusalem, where, according to the prophets, the Messiah would inaugurate the new era.[39] In the crowded slums of the lower city, the Twelve preached the good news to tradesmen, laborers, porters, butchers, dyers, and donkey drivers—"the lost sheep of the House of Israel."[40] In an urban setting that was quite alien to these uprooted peasants, they tried to reproduce the alternative communities Jesus had established in the villages of Galilee:

> The whole community of believers was united in heart and soul. Not one of them claimed any possessions as his own; everything was held in common. With great power the apostles bore witness to the resurrection of the Lord Jesus, and all were held in high esteem. There was never a needy person among them, because those who had property in land or houses would sell it, bring the proceeds of the sale and lay them at the feet of the apostles to be distributed to any who were in need.[41]

The Twelve also began to preach to Greek-speaking immigrants from the diaspora, who had settled in Jerusalem to live a more authentic Jewish life. One of these diaspora Jews was Paul, who, Luke says, came from Tarsus in Cilicia. At first he was hostile to the Jesus movement, but eventually he would take the momentous step of bringing the gospel not only to the lost sheep of Israel but to the pagan nations as well.

I published my first book about Paul in 1983, at the very beginning of my career. *The First Christian* accompanied a six-part television series, which I wrote and presented. At the beginning of this project, I had thought that this was my chance to show how Paul had damaged Christianity and ruined the original, loving teaching of Jesus. Paul is an apostle whom many love to hate; he has been castigated as a misogynist, a supporter of slavery, a virulent authoritarian, and bitterly hostile to Jews and Judaism. When I started to study his writings in a first-century context, however, it did not take me long to realize that this was an untenable view. In fact, as I followed in his footsteps during the filming, I grew not only to admire but also to feel a strong affinity with this difficult, brilliant, and vulnerable man.

One of the first things I discovered was that Paul did not write all the letters attributed to him in the New Testament. Only seven of them are judged by scholars to be authentic: 1 Thessalonians, Galatians, 1 and 2 Corinthians, Philippians, Philemon, and Romans. The rest—Colossians, Ephesians, 2 Thessalonians, 1 and 2 Timothy, and Titus, known as the Deutero-Pauline letters—were written in his name after his death, some as late as the second century. These were not forgeries in our sense; it was common in the ancient world to write under the pseudonym of an admired sage or philosopher. These posthumous epistles tried to rein Paul in and make his radical teachings more acceptable to the Greco-Roman world. It was these later writers who insisted that women be subservient to their husbands and that slaves must obey their masters. It was they who spiritualized Paul's condemnation of the "rulers of this world," claiming that these were demonic powers rather than the ruling aristocracies of the Roman Empire.

Interestingly some feminist theologians find this argument a cop-out; they seem to feel a strong need to blame Paul for the long tradition of Christian misogyny. But it seems irrational for a scholar to close her eyes to critically persuasive data that suggest that Paul could not have written these later texts. Hating Paul seems more important than a just assessment of his work. In fact, as recent research has made clear, Paul took a radical stance on such issues in a way that makes him extremely relevant today. First, scholars such as Richard A. Horsley, Dieter Georgi, and Neil Elliott have shown that, like Jesus, Paul was a lifelong opponent of the structural injustice of the Roman Empire. In the premodern world, all civilizations without exception were based on a surplus of agricultural produce, which was forcibly extracted from the peasantry who were made to live at subsistence level. Thus for five thousand years, about 90 percent of the population was reduced to serfdom in order to support a small privileged class of aristocrats and their retainers. Yet, sociological historians point out, without this iniquitous arrangement, it is unlikely that the human species would have advanced beyond a primitive level, since it created a privileged class with the leisure to develop the arts and sciences that were essential to progress. It was also found, paradoxical as this may seem, that a great tributary empire like Rome was the best way to keep the peace, because it kept smaller, rival aristocracies from endlessly fighting one another to acquire more arable land. In the premodern world, when social unrest that damaged the harvest could cause thousands of deaths, anarchy was greatly feared, and an emperor like Augustus was hailed by most people with relief. Nevertheless, in every culture, there were always voices like Jesus's and Paul's that rose in protest against this institutionalized injustice. Today Paul would probably have been a fierce critic of the global market we have created in which there is such a huge imbalance of wealth and power.

Second, all his life Paul struggled to transcend the barriers of ethnicity, class, and gender that, sadly, are still socially divisive in the twenty-first century. So it is important to set the record straight. His famous experience on the road to Damascus was in large part a discovery that the laws that separated Jews from gentiles—laws that he had championed and promoted all his life—had been abrogated by God. Like Jesus, he would always insist that in the Kingdom of God, everybody must be allowed to eat at the same table. In our secularized world, we no longer place such emphasis on rules of ritual purity; but racism and class divisions are still a noxious force even in what used to be called the Free World. Again, Paul would have vehemently rejected such prejudice, just as Jesus did. Jesus continuously and provocatively ate dinner with "sinners," touched those who were ritually impure and contagiously sick, crossed social boundaries, and consorted with people despised by the establishment.

There is, therefore, much that we can learn from Paul. In *The First Christian,* I relied heavily on the Acts of the Apostles, traditionally believed to have been written by St. Luke, the third evangelist. But Acts is no longer regarded as historically reliable. Luke certainly had access to some authentic traditions, but as he could have been writing as late as the second century, he did not always understand them. He also had an entirely different agenda from Paul. Writing after the Jewish War against Rome, which had resulted in the tragic destruction of Jerusalem and its temple, he was anxious to show that the Jesus movement did not share the widespread Jewish hostility to Rome. In his narrative, therefore, he consistently shows Roman officials responding respectfully and appreciatively to Paul and makes the local Jewish communities responsible for his frequent expulsion from the cities in which he evangelized. Paul, we shall see, had a very different perspective.

In this book, therefore, I rely mainly on Paul's seven authentic letters. There is a great deal that will always remain obscure: We will never learn whether Paul, who made a point of emphasizing his single status, was ever married. We know nothing about his childhood or education, have no details about the five occasions when he was flogged in synagogues, his three shipwrecks (including a night and a day when he was adrift on the open sea), the time he was stoned, or his dangerous encounters with brigands.[42] And despite the legends that have accrued over the centuries, we do not know in any detail how or when he died. But his letters bring him to life and are an extraordinary record of the passions that drove this man to change the world.

Note: It is not accurate to speak of early Christianity as a separate religious tradition. Until well into the second century, it was regarded both by outsiders and members of the Jesus movement as a sect within Judaism. Jesus's followers would not begin to call themselves "Christians" until the end of the first century, and the term "Christianity" occurs only three times in the New Testament.[43] I have also avoided calling the early communities of the Jesus movement "churches," because this term inevitably evokes imagery of spires, pews, hymnbooks, and global hierarchical organizations that simply did not exist in Paul's day. Instead, I prefer to use the Greek *ekklesia* (later translated "church"), which, like "synagogue" refers to an assembly of people, a community or congregation.

I

Damascus

LUKE'S ACCOUNT of the descent of the Spirit on the
Jewish festival of Pentecost may not be historically reliable but it certainly expresses the tumultuous character of
the early Jesus movement.[1] The twelve apostles and members of
Jesus's family, he tells us, were at prayer in their Jerusalem lodging when they suddenly heard a roaring sound, like a driving
wind; flames appeared and rested over the heads of each one of
them. Filled with the Spirit, they began to speak in different languages and rushed outside to address a crowd of Jewish pilgrims
from all over the diaspora, each one of whom heard them speaking in his native tongue. The apostles' demeanor was so wild
that some of the spectators thought they were drunk. Peter reassured them: These men, he explained, were simply filled with
the Spirit of God. This was how the prophet Joel had described
the Last Days, which had been set in motion by Jesus, a man revealed to Israel by miracles, portents, and signs. But, Peter told
his large Jewish audience, by the "deliberate will and plan of
God he was given into your power, and you killed him, using
heathen men to crucify him." Yet God had raised Jesus to a glorious life in the heavenly world, thus fulfilling David's prophecy
in the psalm that begins: "The Lord said to my Lord, 'Sit at my
right hand until I make your enemies your footstool.'"[2] Israel
must now acknowledge the crucified Jesus as Lord and Messiah;

if people repented, were baptized, and separated themselves from "this crooked age," they too would receive the Spirit and share Jesus's victory.[3]

Overnight Jesus, the man, had been forever transformed. After seeing him standing at God's right hand, his disciples had immediately begun to search the scriptures to help them understand what God had done for him. From a very early date they meditated on Psalm 110, which Peter quoted to the crowd. In ancient Israel, this had been sung during the coronation ceremony in the temple, when the newly anointed king, a descendant of David, had been elevated to near-divine status and made a member of the Divine Council of heavenly beings. Another psalm proclaimed that at his coronation the king had been adopted by Yahweh: "You are my son, today I have become your father."[4] The disciples also remembered that Jesus had sometimes spoken of himself as the "son of man," a phrase that took them to Psalm 8, where the wonders of creation had inspired the psalmist to ask why God should have raised a lowly "son of man" to the eminence that, as they had seen with their own eyes, Jesus now enjoyed:

> *You have made him little less than a god,*
> *You have crowned him with glory and splendour,*
> *Made him lord over the work of your hands,*
> *Set all things under his feet.*[5]

Again, the title "son of man" brought to mind the vision of the prophet Daniel, who had seen a mysterious figure "like a son of man" coming to the aid of Israel on the clouds of Heaven: "On him was conferred sovereignty, glory, and kingship, and men of all peoples, languages, and nations became his servants."[6] Jesus, the son of man, the disciples were now convinced, would soon return to rule the world and conquer Israel's oppressors. With truly remarkable speed, the titles "lord" (*kyrios* in Greek), "son of man," and "son of God" were attributed to Jesus, the Messiah, the Christos, and used routinely by all New Testament authors.[7]

The Pentecost story suggests that the gospel had an immediate appeal for Greek-speaking Jews from the diaspora, many of whom joined the community of Jesus's followers. First-century Jerusalem was a cosmopolitan city. Devout Jews came from all over the world to worship in the temple, though they tended to form their own synagogues where they could pray in Greek rather than in Hebrew or the Aramaic dialect used in Judea.[8] Some of them were dedicated to *ioudaismos*, a word that is often translated as "Judaism" or "Jewishness" but which during the Roman period had a more precise significance. The emperors respected the antiquity and morality of Israelite religion and had granted Jewish communities a degree of autonomy in the Greco-Roman cities. But this was often resented by local elites who were smarting under their own loss of independence, so periodically anti-Jewish tension erupted among the townsfolk. To counter this, some Greek-speaking Jews had developed a militant diaspora consciousness that they called *ioudaismos*, a defiant assertion of ancestral tradition combined with a determination to preserve a distinctly Jewish identity and forestall any political threat to their community—resorting to violence, if necessary. Some were even prepared to act as vigilantes to enforce the Torah and defend the honor of Israel. In Jerusalem, these more rigorous Jews were attracted to the Judean sect of the Pharisees, who were committed to a punctilious observance of the Torah. Because they wanted to live in the same way as the priests who served the Divine Presence in the temple, they gave special prominence to the priestly purity laws and the dietary regulations that made Israel "holy" (*qaddosh* in Hebrew), that is, as "separate" and "other," as God himself and utterly distinct from the gentile world.

But other Greek-speaking Jews may have found life in the Holy City disappointing. In the diaspora, many had come to appreciate Hellenistic culture. They tended, therefore, to stress the universality inherent in Jewish monotheism, seeing the One God as the Father of all peoples, who was worshiped under different names. Some also believed that the Torah was not the possession of the Jews alone but that in their own way the ancestral laws of the Greeks and Romans also expressed the will of the One God. Instead of concentrating on ritual minutiae, therefore, these more liberal Jews were drawn to the ethical vision of the prophets, who had emphasized the importance of charity and philanthropy rather than the ceremonial laws of purity and diet. They probably found the Pharisees' preoccupations stifling and petty, and they may also have been offended by the commercial exploitation of pilgrims in the Holy City.[9] So when they heard the Twelve talking about Jesus, they would have been drawn to some of his teachings. For instance, he was said to have been critical of the Pharisees: "You pay tithes of mint and rue and every garden herb but neglect justice and the love of God. It is these you should have practiced, without overlooking the other."[10] They would also have liked the story of Jesus driving the money changers out of the temple as he quoted the words of Isaiah that reflected the universal implications of the cult: "My house shall be called a house of prayer for all nations."[11]

When they joined the Jesus movement, these Greek-speaking Jews continued to pray in their own synagogues. But, Luke tells us, tension broke out between the Aramaic-speaking and Greek-speaking members. According to Acts, it began as a disagreement about the distribution of the food, which the Twelve resolved by appointing seven Greek-speaking deacons to apportion rations to the community so that they themselves could devote more time to prayer and preaching.[12] But Luke's account is full of contradictions, and it is clear that the duties of the seven deacons were not simply domestic. One of them was Stephen, who was a charismatic preacher and miracle worker, while Philip, another of the Seven, led a mission to the non-Jewish regions of Samaria and Gaza.[13] Reading between the lines of Luke's narrative, we can see that the Seven may have been leaders of a separate "Hellene" congregation in the Jesus movement who conducted their own preaching missions and were already reaching out to the gentile world.

In Luke's story, this trivial dispute about food escalated with horrifying speed to a lynching in which Stephen was killed. Some of the diaspora Jews who were committed to *ioudaismos* were incensed by Stephen's liberal preaching and had him dragged before the high priest. At all costs, Stephen had to be stopped. "This fellow is forever saying things against this holy place and against the law. For we have heard him say this Jesus of Nazareth will destroy [the temple] and alter the customs handed down to us by Moses."[14] Luke claims that these were trumped-up charges put forward by false witnesses; yet he makes Stephen give a long speech that does conclude with a defiant rejection of the temple cult. This, as we have seen, was indeed a bone of contention. Stephen's views were shared in part by the Qumran sectarians and by the peasants who refused to pay their tithes. According to the gospels, Jesus had also predicted the temple's destruction.[15] When Stephen finally cried, "Look! I see the heavens opened and the Son of Man standing at the right hand of God," his accusers were filled with rage and, flinging their coats at the feet of a young man named Saul, they hustled Stephen out of the city to stone him. "Saul," Luke ends this tragic tale, "was among those who approved of this execution."[16]

Paul enters the story probably about two years after Jesus's death, in 32/33. We know almost nothing about his early life. It is Luke who tells us that he came originally from Tarsus and was brought by his parents to Jerusalem as a boy. Paul himself would proudly insist on his impeccable Jewish ancestry: "Circumcised on the eighth day, Israelite by race, of the tribe of Benjamin, a

Hebrew born and bred; in my practice of the law a Pharisee, in zeal for religion a persecutor of the church, by the law's standard of righteousness without fault."[17] In the sixteenth century, Martin Luther would claim that Paul had agonized about his inability to fulfill all the "works of the law," but there is no sign of this in Paul's letters. On the contrary, he confidently maintained that he had been a very successful Jew, his Torah observance "without fault." We know very little about Pharisaic practice before the Jewish War; it seems to have been a many-faceted movement with a broad spectrum of beliefs, and even though the Pharisees would later pioneer Rabbinic Judaism, we cannot assume that Paul shared the ideas that the Talmudic rabbis developed after the Jewish War. Paul probably attended a Greek-speaking Jewish school in Jerusalem. He spoke Greek fluently, had studied the Hebrew Scriptures in Greek translation, and had also mastered the arts of rhetoric. But his upbringing would not have been narrowly religious. Ever since the second century BCE, Pharisees had been political activists, ready to die and sometimes to kill for their convictions. In the early first century, some of them seem to have functioned as a pressure group, aggressively promoting *ioudaismos* and punishing dissenters like Stephen in order to hold Jewish society together under the strain of Roman occupation.[18]

Paul made it clear that he had been a particularly zealous Pharisee: "In the practice of ioudaismos, I outstripped most of my Jewish contemporaries by my boundless devotion to the traditions of my ancestors."[19] Where some Jews, distressed by the political crises of Roman occupation and excessive taxation, either turned to charismatic teachers like John the Baptist or engaged in other forms of nonviolent protest, others believed that these disasters were God's punishment for their failure to observe the Torah. They concluded that instead of defying the Roman authorities and endangering the Jewish community, it was better to devote themselves to observing the commandments stringently, trusting that God would ultimately reward their fidelity. Only thus could they hasten the Messianic Age in which God would restore the honor of his people.[20] This was probably Paul's view; he seems to have been a recognized Pharisaic leader and may have instructed diaspora Jews residing in Jerusalem to resist assimilation to the Greco-Roman ethos and avoid any anti-Roman activity that might lead to military reprisals. The biblical hero of these more rigorous Pharisees was the priest Phinehas. During their years in the wilderness, the Israelites had succumbed to the worship of local gods and Yahweh had punished them with a plague that killed twenty-four thousand of his people. But Phinehas had turned back God's wrath by killing one of these sinners and his Midianite wife and was praised for his zeal for God's law.[21] It was in this spirit that Paul would persecute the communities of Jesus's followers.

He seems, however, to have had no problem with the Twelve and the Judean followers of Jesus, who were more loyal to ancestral tradition. According to Luke, far from denouncing the cult, like Stephen, they worshipped together every day in the temple.[22] Indeed, the revered Pharisee Gamaliel, whose views were more liberal than Paul's, is said to have advised the Sanhedrin to leave the Jesus movement alone: If it was of human origin, it would break up of its own accord like other recent protest groups.[23] But for Paul, the Hellenistic followers of Jesus were insulting everything he believed to be most sacred, and he greatly feared that their devotion to a man executed so recently by the Roman authorities would put the entire community at risk. Paul himself had never had any dealings with Jesus before his death, but he would have been horrified to learn that Jesus had desecrated the temple and argued that some of God's laws were more important than others. For a Pharisee with extreme views, like Paul, a Jew who did not observe every single one of the commandments was endangering the Jewish people, since God could punish such infidelity as severely as he had punished the ancient Israelites in the time of Moses.

But above all, Paul was scandalized by the outrageous idea of a crucified Messiah.[24] How could a convicted criminal possibly restore the dignity and liberty of Israel? This was an utter travesty, a *scandalon* or "stumbling block." The Torah was adamant that such a man was hopelessly polluted: "If a man guilty of a capital offense is put to death and you hang him on a gibbet, his body must not remain on the tree overnight; you must bury him the same day, for the one who has been hanged is accursed of God, and you must not defile the land that Yahweh your God has given you."[25] True, his followers insisted that Jesus had been buried on the day of his death, but Paul was well aware that most Roman soldiers had little respect for Jewish sensibilities and might well have left Jesus's body hanging on his cross to be consumed by birds of prey. Even though this was no fault of his own, such a man was an abomination and had defiled the Land of Israel.[26] To imagine that these desecrated remains had been raised to the right hand of God was abhorrent, unthinkable, and blasphemous. It impugned the honor of God and his people and would delay the longed-for coming of the Messiah, so it was, Paul believed, his duty to eradicate this sect.

Paul played only a passive role in the stoning of Stephen, but when the Hellenes continued to spread their blasphemous ideas, he went on the offensive: "he entered house after house, seizing men and women and sending them to prison."[27] He did not shrink from brute force and would later remind his followers of "how savagely I persecuted the church of God and tried to destroy [*eporthoun*] it," the Greek verb implying utter annihilation.[28] Some of his victims may have been condemned to thirtynine lashes in the synagogue; others may have been beaten up or even lynched like Stephen, until finally the Greek-speaking community of Jesus's followers had been eliminated from Jerusalem. As Luke explained, this was "a time of persecution for the congregation in Jerusalem, and all *except the apostles* were scattered over the country district of Judea and Samaria."[29] While the Aramaic-speaking congregations clustered around the Twelve were left unscathed, the expelled Hellenes began their mission in the diaspora, making their way "to Phoenicia, Cyprus, and Antioch, bringing the message of Jesus to Jews only, and to no others."[30]

Some became active in the synagogues of Damascus, and when he heard this, Luke tells us that Paul, still "breathing murderous threats against the Lord's disciples," applied to the high priest for permission to arrest them and bring them back to Jerusalem for punishment.[31] It is, however, most unlikely that the high priest would have intervened in the affairs of a diaspora community, though it is possible that Paul was dispatched by some of the more zealous Pharisees to safeguard the Jewish community in Damascus, whose position at this time was extremely precarious.[32] Thirty years later, at the beginning of the Jewish War against Rome, all the Jews of Damascus would be rounded up on a blanket charge of sedition, herded into the gymnasium, and slaughtered within an hour. The news that a messianic pretender executed by a Roman governor had been raised to life and would soon return to destroy his enemies could endanger the whole community.[33] Paul set out to prevent this catastrophe, only to have his life thrown off course by a wholly unexpected experience on the road to Damascus.[34]

Luke says that just before Paul reached the city he was thrown from his horse and blinded by a light from the sky. He heard a voice asking: "Saul, Saul, why are you persecuting me?" When Paul asked who the speaker was, the voice replied, "I am Jesus, whom you are persecuting," and instructed him to await further directions in Damascus.[35] Luke certainly expressed an essential aspect of Paul's conversion: He had suddenly discovered the terrible paradox of his position. Later he would try to explain the dilemma of the die-hard fanatic he had once been: "The good which I want to do, I fail to do, but what I do is the wrong which is against my will!"[36] Paul had been doing his best to hasten the coming of the Messiah; that was the "good" that he was trying to do. But in an overwhelming moment of truth, he realized that Jesus's followers were absolutely right and that his persecution of their community had actually impeded the arrival of the Messianic Age. As if this were not enough, his violence had broken the fundamental principles of the Torah: love of God and love of neighbor. In his excessive ardor for the law's integrity, he had forgotten God's stern command: "Thou shalt not kill." "In my inmost self, I delight in the law of God, but I perceive in my actions a different law, fighting against the law that my mind approves," he would reflect later on his predicament. "Wretched creature that I am, who is there to rescue me from this state of death? Who but God?"[37] By showing him the tortured and polluted body of Jesus, standing in glory at his right hand, God had indeed delivered Paul from this deadly conundrum, and Paul would spend the rest of his life working out the implications of an insight that was at once devastating — because it snatched Paul away from everything that had hitherto given meaning to his life — but also profoundly liberating.

But in some respects, Luke's view of the Damascus experience was very different from Paul's. In the Acts of the Apostles, Luke calls it a "vision" (*orama*), an "ecstasy" (*ekstasis*), or an "apparition" (*optasia*), but when he described the encounters of Jesus's disciples with the risen Christ in his gospel, he did not use any of these words. These earlier sightings, Luke believed, had been objective, physical events. Jesus had walked, talked, and eaten with them just as he did before the crucifixion. Paul's "vision" experience bore no resemblance to this. Indeed, Luke went out of his way to explain that Paul did not actually *see* Jesus at all; because he was blinded by the light, he only heard his voice. In short, Luke did not regard Paul as a witness to the resurrection in the same way as the Twelve. But for Paul, the most important thing about his experience was that he actually *did* see the Lord and that Jesus appeared to him in exactly the same way as he had appeared to the Twelve.[38] It was a controversial claim and would often be contested. For Paul, an apostle was someone who had seen the risen Christ. "Am I not an apostle?" he would demand. "Have I not seen the Lord?"[39] In a letter to his converts in Corinth, he recounted what had become a major tradition in the Jesus movement, listing in order the Easter sightings of Peter, the Twelve, the five hundred, and James, concluding: "Last of all he appeared to me too; it was as though I was born when no one expected it."[40] This was not a conversion in the usual sense, since Paul was not changing his religion. He would regard himself as a Jew for the rest of his life and he understood the Damascus revelation in entirely Jewish terms: He had been called in just the same way as God had called Isaiah; God had selected Paul, like Jeremiah, when he was still in his mother's womb.[41]

In Luke's account in the Acts of the Apostles, Jesus appeared to his disciples for a limited period of forty days, after which his body ascended to Heaven. So Luke believed that Paul's vision, which happened years after the ascension, was essentially distinct from the Easter visions of the Twelve.[42] But Luke was writing decades after the Damascus experience. When Paul was dictating his letters in the 50s, the stories of Jesus's physical meetings with the Twelve had not yet become part of the tradition. Paul knew nothing about the forty-day period and had never heard of Jesus's ascension as a separate occurrence, since in these first years, the resurrection and ascension formed a single event: God had raised Jesus's body out of the tomb and conveyed it immediately to the heavenly world. Writing in the late 60s, Mark, the first evangelist, still saw the resurrection that way. He described the women going to anoint Jesus's body after the Sabbath, three days after his death, only to find that the tomb was empty. "He has been raised," an angel informed them; "he is not here," and the women "ran away from the tomb, trembling with amazement." Mark leaves the reader with unanswered questions: "They said nothing to anybody, for they were afraid."[43]

Paul was indeed a mystic; as far as we know he was the first Jewish mystic to record his experiences. Early Jewish mysticism was not a peaceful, yogic activity; a Jewish visionary experienced an ascent through the heavens until he reached God's throne, bringing back terrifying news about God's imminent judgment of the world.[44] Paul described a celestial flight exactly like this in another letter to the Corinthians, and some scholars believe that he might be describing his Damascus experience in this passage.[45] But others disagree. They point out that Paul is hesitant, puzzled, and ambiguous about his ascent to the third heaven, but in his letter to the Galatians, he writes quite straightforwardly about his Damascus encounter with Jesus, which seems to have been quite different.[46] In the celestial flight experience, a Jewish mystic induced his visions, engaging in lengthy preparations — fasting and sitting for hours with his head between his knees, murmuring the divine praises.[47] But there was no such preparation for the Damascus vision, which came to Paul out of the blue, "when no one expected it."

The American scholar Alan F. Segal helps us to understand how Jesus's earliest followers conceptualized their visions of the risen Christ.[48] Jesus's physical ascension was not without precedent: Adam, Enoch, Moses, and Elijah were all said to have been carried bodily into Heaven; mystics saw them there sitting on golden thrones. After the prophet Ezekiel had been deported to Babylon in 597, he had a vision of Yahweh that made an indelible impression on the Jewish imagination. He had seen the God of Israel, leaving the Holy Land and traveling to join the exiles in a war chariot drawn by four strange beasts. High above their heads, Ezekiel saw something that defied normal categorization. It "looked like a sapphire, it was shaped like a throne and high up on this throne was a being that looked like a man." This humanlike figure was surrounded by a nimbus of fire and light that "looked like the glory [*kavod*] of Yahweh."[49] One could never see God himself—that lay beyond human capacity—but it was possible to glimpse God's "glory," a kind of afterglow of the divine presence adapted to the limitations of human perception. In Israelite tradition, the "being that looked like a man" in Ezekiel's vision was sometimes linked with the angel who had guided the people of Israel through the wilderness to the Promised Land. "Give heed to him," God had commanded them, "for my *name* is in him."[50] This cluster of images helped Paul and the Twelve to understand the Easter event; it also explains how their perception of what had happened to Jesus was so widely and rapidly accepted by so many Jews at a very early stage in the Jesus movement.

In the risen body of Jesus on his heavenly throne, his disciples had seen the *kavod* of God: "We saw his glory, such glory as befits the Father's only Son, full of grace and truth."[51] In one of his letters, Paul quoted a very early hymn that associated the risen Jesus, the Christos, with God's "name" and God's "glory." The crucified Messiah had given limited human beings an astonishing glimpse of the divine. He had been elevated to this extraordinary eminence by "emptying himself," making himself nothing, even to the extent of accepting death on a cross: "Therefore God raised him to the heights and bestowed on him the name above all names," so that every tongue should cry "Jesus Christ is Lord [*Kyrios*]! to the glory of God, the Father."[52]

Instead of calling his encounter with Jesus in Damascus a vision, Paul experienced it as an *apocalupsis*, a "revelation."[53] Like the Latin *revelatio,* the Greek *apocalupsis* meant "unveiling." A veil was, as it were, suddenly stripped away from a reality that had been there all the time, but which we had not seen before. At Damascus, it seemed to Paul as though scales had been removed from his eyes and he had an entirely new insight into the nature of God. For Paul the Pharisee, God was utterly pure and free of all contamination. Like a priest who stood in the presence of God in the temple, a Pharisee had to purify himself if he had any physical contact with a corpse, because the God that was life itself could have nothing to do with the corruption of death. But when Paul saw that God had embraced Jesus's filthy, degraded body and raised it to the highest place in Heaven, he realized that in fact God had an entirely different set of values. In honoring Jesus in this way, God had signaled a change in the way he approached humanity. To a man sentenced to death by Roman law, God had said: "Sit at my right hand and I will make your enemies a footstool for you." He had raised a corpse that the Torah declared to be especially polluting, indeed accursed, saying to Jesus: "You are my son; today I have become your father." The old rules no longer applied. Who now was high and who low? Who was really close to God and who far from him?

When Paul described his Damascus experience to his disciples in Galatia, he said only that God had chosen "to reveal his Son to me for the exact purpose that I might preach him among the gentiles."[54] When Paul saw the ritually defiled body of Jesus at God's right hand, he understood exactly why he had received this mission. He had chosen to live in the Holy Land because the gentile world was unclean. Jews tended to regard the non-Jewish nations as impure and morally inferior. But in raising Jesus, God had shown that he did not judge by these earthly standards and that he stood by people who were despised and denigrated by the rules and laws of this world. God had no favorites. It was now time to bring the knowledge of the One God to the pagan nations.

Antioch

W E NOW ENTER a period of about fifteen years in Paul's life about which we know very little. Luke skirts over them and Paul himself gives us only the barest outline, perhaps because they ended so bitterly that the memory was painful. Immediately after his Damascus vision, he explained: "Without consulting a single person, without going up to Jerusalem to see those who were apostles before me, I went off to Arabia."[1] In this letter, Paul was anxious to emphasize his independence of the Twelve and the Jerusalem community. He always insisted that he had been appointed to his mission by Christ himself and had no need of endorsement by the Jerusalem leaders. His insistence on this point suggests that such deliberate avoidance of the Twelve was widely regarded as strange, even suspicious. But Paul had good reason to believe that he would be persona non grata in the Holy City. Members of the Jesus movement would almost certainly have found his sudden conversion suspect, and he might also have feared reprisals from his former Pharisee friends for his apparent apostasy. So he set off immediately to the gentile world to fulfill his mission.

But why Arabia rather than the cities of Phoenicia or Palmyra? There were good practical reasons for this choice. The Kingdom of Nabataea in the southern Palestine region, in what is now Jordan and northwestern Saudi Arabia, was Israel's most powerful neighbor. When Paul arrived there in about 33/34, it had acquired great wealth by carefully controlling the trade routes from southern Arabia and the Persian Gulf that conveyed such luxury goods as spices, gold, pearls, and rare medicines to the Mediterranean world. Under King Aretas IV, the city of Petra, carved out of reddish sandstone, had become a local marvel. As it had a significant Jewish population, Paul probably preached in some of the synagogues in the larger Nabataean towns to the "Godfearers" (*theosebes*), gentiles who admired the Jewish faith, attended services, and enjoyed the scripture readings, but had not gone through the lengthy and difficult process of full conversion. Political and economic relations with Judea were good; the Arabs were thought to be the descendants of Ishmael, Abraham's elder son by his concubine Hagar.[2] They were, therefore, kindred tribes, and for their part the Arabs believed that they were members of the Abrahamic family and circumcised their sons. The prophet Isaiah and Jeremiah had both predicted that at the end of time, Nabataea would be among those nations that would come to acknowledge Yahweh in Jerusalem,[3] so Paul may have thought that Arabia was as good a place as any to start his mission.[4]

He tells us nothing about his activities there, so we can only speculate about these years. He must have spent much time in thought and prayer, working out the implications of the Damascus experience, and it is tempting to suggest ways in which his stay in Arabia influenced him. For the rest of his life as a missionary, Paul would support himself by working with his own hands,[5] and Luke claims, on the basis of a reliable tradition, that he was either a tentmaker or leatherworker (*skenopoios*).[6] The Mishnah would later recommend Torah students to combine their study with a practical trade, so it was often assumed that Paul had learned his craft during his apprenticeship with Gamaliel, whom Luke claims to have been his teacher.[7] But this rabbinic practice is not attested until the mid-second century.

Tent making was especially important in Arabia, where the local Bedouin were known as *sarakenoi,* "tent dwellers." If he did
indeed acquire this craft in Arabia, Paul would have learned exactly how to cut the leather and the intricate art of stitching the
pieces together so that the tent remained waterproof. He would
have spent hours every day on a stool bent over his workbench,
his hands becoming so calloused and stiff that his handwriting
may have become exceptionally large.[8]

This profession enabled Paul to remain economically independent and sometimes even provided him with a place to
live.[9] It was also the context of much of his mission. The great
masters often depicted Paul preaching to large crowds in beautiful colonnades and grand lecture halls, but we should probably picture him expounding the gospel in his workshop. Tent
making was quiet work, and it would have been quite possible
for Paul to discuss his ideas about Jesus and the Kingdom with
fellow workers and customers. Workshops were often conven-
iently situated in the *agora* ("marketplace") or in the back room
of a shop. Paul did not have time for public lectures, because
he worked long hours. "You remember, my friends," he wrote to
the Thessalonians, "night and day we worked for a living."[10] It
was customary for an artisan to rise before sunrise so as to use all
the hours of daylight. Apart from the Sabbath, Paul would have
been at work all and every day, and if they wanted to see him,
his disciples would have to come to his bench.

Not many of the apostles supported themselves in this way,
and some of Paul's opponents believed that by classing himself
with the lower echelons of society, he brought the gospel into
disrepute. But after Damascus, Paul wanted to transcend such
distinctions. Unlike many of Jesus's disciples, he had been born
into the social elite and was able to devote his life to study, a luxury that was possible only for the leisured classes. In all premodern societies, the upper classes were chiefly distinguished from
the rest of the population by their ability to live without work-

ing.[11] The cultural historian Thorstein Veblen explains that in such societies, "labor comes to be associated . . . with weakness and subjection." Work was not only "disreputable . . . but morally impossible for the noble freeborn man."[12] Artisans were often treated with contempt, which, given Paul's relatively privileged upbringing, must have been especially hard. But by deliberately abandoning this lifestyle and living in solidarity with common laborers, Paul was practicing a daily *kenosis* or "self-emptying," similar to Jesus's when he "emptied himself to assume the condition of a slave."[13] Indeed, Paul said that by taking up this menial occupation, he had in fact enslaved himself.[14] It was a hard life. Paul said that he and his fellow workers were often "overworked and sleepless,"[15] and went "hungry, thirsty, and in rags," "wearing ourselves out by earning a living by our own hands" and "treated as the scum of the earth, as the dregs of humanity."[16]

Living in Arabia may also have made Paul newly aware of the importance of Abraham, who would play an important role in his theology.[17] Many Jews located Mount Sinai (where Moses had received the Torah from God) in south Nabataea. The fact that Sinai was near Hagra, its second-largest city, made a great impression on Paul, because the city may have been named after Hagar, Abraham's concubine. Henceforth Paul would associate Hagar with the Torah, her status as a slave symbolizing the bondage of the Mosaic Law from which, he believed, Christ had liberated him.[18] When he looked back on his life as a Pharisaic vigilante, Paul believed that he had been in thrall to what he called "sin." He would always adamantly deny that the law was identical to sin; no, he insisted, the Torah was "a good thing" but, despite his punctilious observance of the commandments, he had remained "a prisoner under the law of sin which controls my conduct."[19] He was, therefore, "a slave to sin," because he had found it impossible to do what he knew, in his heart, to be right.[20] For Paul sin was a demonic power before which we were virtually helpless. Today we might link his concept of "sin" with the instinctual reptilian drives that neurologists have located in the deepest part of our brains, without which our species would not have survived. These impulses impel us to flee any danger, fight for territory and status, grab whatever resources are available, and perpetuate our genes. The "me first" drives that we have inherited from our reptilian ancestors are automatic, immediate, and powerful; they inform all our activities, including our religion, and are extremely difficult to resist. Paul would look back at his former zeal for the law as depraved, because he had been possessed by an egotistic chauvinism that had impelled him to fight, destroy, and even kill his fellow Jews to preserve the honor and status of his people.

But if Hagar represented his former self, her husband, Abraham, symbolized the way forward. According to Jewish tradition, Abraham had once traveled along the spice route, making a ritualized circuit of the land that God had promised his descendants.[21] Now as he traveled in Arabia, Paul found himself walking in Abraham's footsteps. Long before the Torah had been revealed to Moses on Mount Sinai, God had declared Abraham to be a just man because of his trust (*pistis*) in God.[22] Before Abraham had been circumcised, God had promised that all the nations of the world would find blessing in him.[23] As he thought about his mission to the gentile world, Paul would naturally have seen Abraham as a pivotal figure. Abraham had not been born a Jew, yet he became the ancestor of the Jewish people and so he was in some sense both Jew and gentile. Like Abraham, Paul had also been instructed by God to leave his former way of life and travel in alien lands; he too had been called to found a new kind of family—one that would include both Jews and gentiles.[24] Paul may have known that John the Baptist had warned his Jewish hearers not to rely on their physical descent from Abraham,[25] and that Jesus had predicted that when the Kingdom was established, gentiles would come from afar to eat at the same table as Abraham, Isaac, and Jacob.[26] Both had hinted at Paul's future mission to the pagan world through which God's ancient promise to Abraham would be fulfilled.

But Paul was in Arabia at a most inauspicious moment. In 34 CE, Herod Antipas had encroached into Nabataean territory, where he established an Israelite enclave south of the Dead Sea. But in a surprise attack, King Aretas wiped out the Herodian mercenaries there and Antipas eventually fell from favor in Rome and was exiled to Lugdunum (now Lyons) in the province of Gaul. Many Jews saw his downfall as God's punishment for his execution of John the Baptist, while Jesus's followers were convinced that it heralded the imminent arrival of the Kingdom. As a result of this political turmoil, Paul may have been obliged to return to Damascus, where, it seems, his subversive preaching came to the attention of King Aretas, who was now Rome's principal client in the region. Paul had to flee for his life, and his friends helped him to escape by lowering him down the city wall in a basket.[27]

Once he was safely outside Aretas's territory, Paul spent two weeks in Jerusalem as the guest of Peter. It was a cautious, perhaps even a clandestine visit, since Paul may still have feared the vengeance of former victims and colleagues. He was lying low: "I saw none of the other apostles, except James, the Lord's brother," he would later tell the Galatians.[28] At this point, Peter was still the undisputed leader of the Jerusalem congregation, but James may have headed the more conservative wing of the Jesus movement, which observed the Torah more rigorously. It would be fascinating to know what they talked about. Peter would certainly have taught Paul many of the traditional stories about Jesus, and Paul may have shared with Peter his new insights about the significance of Abraham. As the only intellectual in the movement, he would have been able to express his ideas forcefully and may have exerted a considerable influence on Peter, who would come to accept some of his views.[29]

At the end of the fortnight, Paul returned to the diaspora and would not visit Jerusalem again for fourteen years. Once back on the road, he journeyed to Cilicia, but again we know nothing about his mission there.[30] He may have continued to follow Abraham's legendary circuit of the Promised Land, traveling in his wake along the Mediterranean coast and turning eastward into the Taurus region until he reached the River Euphrates.[31] According to Jewish topography, on the other side of the Taurus Mountains was the territory that had been assigned to Noah's youngest son, Japheth, after the flood. One day Paul would venture into this foreign realm, but at this point he preferred to remain in the land of Noah's oldest son, Shem, the ancestor of the Semitic peoples.[32] He may have founded some churches in Cilicia, but we have no evidence of this. Then in the year 40 he was summoned to Antioch, the third-largest city in the eastern empire.

According to Luke, the movement had made great strides in Antioch, where the preaching of the Hellenes, who had been expelled from Jerusalem, had attracted a large number of Godfearers, who were exceptionally numerous in this city.[33] Unlike Rome or Alexandria, Antioch had no separate Jewish quarter, so the Jewish congregations were scattered throughout the city. Antiochenes were curious about religion; many had been drawn to Judaism, and when they visited the household congregations of the Messiah's people, many of them felt at home. Their native traditions were full of *entheos* ("possession by a god"), so they would have thoroughly enjoyed the noisy, enthusiastic meetings of the Jesus believers, who, under the inspiration of the Spirit, were moved to glossolalia ("speaking in tongues"), visions, ecstasies, and inspired prophetic utterance. The Godfearers also discovered that once they were baptized, they became full members of the congregation instead of remaining second-class citizens in the mainstream synagogues.

When news of these conversions reached Jerusalem, the Twelve were naturally intrigued but felt that a degree of caution was necessary. Peter had baptized Godfearers without insisting that they be circumcised—but not in such large numbers. Perhaps this was another sign that the Kingdom was at hand, for the prophets had predicted that in the Last Days, gentile peoples from all over the world would finally acknowledge the God of Israel. But how authentic was the faith of these Syrians? Were they still tainted by their old idolatrous practices? When they prophesied or spoke in tongues, were they truly inspired by the Spirit or did they attribute their charisma to one of their native gods? Was it really feasible for Jews and uncircumcised gentiles to live and worship together? How could gentiles eat with observant Jews if they did not observe the dietary laws? The Twelve decided to send Barnabas to investigate, because, as a Jew from Cyprus who spoke Aramaic and Greek, he spanned both worlds.[34] As a diaspora Jew, Barnabas was aware that mixed congregations of Jews and gentiles were quite common outside Judea. In fact, the diaspora synagogues often discouraged Godfearers from becoming full proselytes, because the Roman authorities tended to become alarmed if there were too many conversions.[35] But when he arrived in Antioch, Barnabas may have decided that the gentile converts needed a more thorough grounding in the Hebrew Scriptures and that Paul, a learned Pharisee who had been engaged in the gentile mission for years, was the obvious person to teach them. So, Luke tells us, Barnabas "went off to Tarsus to look for Saul; and when he had found him, he brought him to Antioch."[36]

Yet again, Paul arrived at a particularly difficult and, indeed, dangerous moment. The previous year, the emperor Caligula, who had declared himself a god on his accession, had decreed that his statue be erected in the Jewish temple. Petronius, governor of Antioch, was sent to Palestine to install it, but when he arrived at the port of Ptolemais, he found the surrounding countryside crowded with thousands of Jewish peasants and townsfolk who were protesting against this imperial order. They told Petronius that if the idol was brought into the temple, they would refuse to harvest the crops, which, Petronius explained to the emperor, would make it impossible to collect the annual tribute. There was a standoff, which was greatly resented in Antioch, where Caligula was extremely popular. His father, Germanicus, had died in the city and had been revered by the people, and when Antioch was devastated by an earthquake in 37, Caligula had funded the reconstruction. When the news that Petronius had been foiled by Jewish activists reached the city, there were riots: Synagogues were destroyed and many Jews were killed. When Caligula was assassinated in the year after Paul's arrival, Jews in Alexandria and Antioch rose up in revolt. The new emperor Claudius (r. 41–54 CE) suppressed these uprisings but reaffirmed the Jews' traditional rights, and a precarious peace was restored.

Luke tells us that Antioch was the place where the followers of Jesus were first called "Christians."[37] It is possible that during the riots that broke out after Caligula's death, the imperial officials in Antioch began to call those Jews who venerated the Messiah crucified by Pilate *Christianoi,* in order to distinguish them from the *Herodianoi,* the Jews who believed that Herod Agrippa, the new pro-Roman Jewish king in Judea, would restore the fortunes of Israel.[38] The *Christianoi* may, therefore, already have been regarded as potential dissidents. Paul was doubtless appalled by Caligula's divine pretensions and dismayed by the ubiquity of the emperor cult in Antioch. Sacrifice had been offered to Julius Caesar and the goddess Roma in the city since the time of Augustus, and the emperor Tiberius

(r. 14–37 CE) had claimed divine honors there for himself and his brother, Drusus. But Paul would probably have discouraged the *Christianoi* from taking part in the uprising after Caligula's death; he always told his disciples to "live quietly" until the Messiah returned to establish his kingdom — an event that he firmly believed would happen in his own lifetime.[39]

For a whole year after his arrival, Paul and Barnabas worked together to establish the Antioch congregation on a firmer footing. In Antioch, if not in Jerusalem, they were both regarded as full apostles on a par with the Twelve — Barnabas because he had been involved in the movement from the very beginning and may even have known Jesus, and Paul because of the Damascus commission.[40] In Antioch Paul was not an innovator but seems to have preserved the institutions set up by the Twelve at the start of the movement. Baptism remained the movement's initiation rite. In this experimental community of Jews and gentiles, the baptismal cry that greeted each new member as he emerged from the water had a special significance: "No more Jew or Greek, slave or freeman, male or female!"[41] This attitude may have been shared by Jesus himself, and the Hellenes who had brought the gospel to Antioch had long interpreted Judaism in a way that brought out the universalism inherent in monotheism. In the diaspora, the issue of circumcision for the converted pagans was not as problematic as in the Jewish homeland.[42]

Paul had also inherited the tradition of the Lord's Supper from the Twelve; his description of this celebration tallies exactly with Mark's in the earliest extant gospel, which is based on traditions associated with Peter.[43] This was a real meal in which everybody ate his fill, but it was also a "remembrance"; bread and wine were blessed, just as they had been at the last meal that Jesus had eaten with the Twelve before his arrest, so the Supper was a ritualized reenactment of his death. But because the focus of worship was no longer the Torah but the Messiah, this was a breach with Jewish custom, as were the enthusiastic manifestations of the Spirit.[44] All the leaders of the movement in Antioch, including Paul, were prophets as well as teachers.[45] When they deliberated about community policy, they fasted and prayed like other Jewish mystics, possibly with their heads between their knees, waiting for inspiration.[46] The eruption of the Spirit in glossolalia, inspired utterance, and healings showed that the divine power unleashed by Jesus's glorification was now an active presence in the world.[47]

The Antioch congregation also conducted missions in Cyprus, Pamphylia, and southern Galatia in which Paul may or may not have participated. Luke's account of what is often called Paul's first missionary journey, which is full of legendary material, is clearly not historical.[48] The story of Sergius Paulus, governor of Cyprus, accepting the gospel stands in stark contrast to the "jealous resentment" of the local Jewish communities — a bias that reflects Luke's constant concern to dissociate the movement from Judaism.[49] But these tales may also portray the general thrust of years of preaching by now unknown missionaries as the movement gradually spread outward from Antioch into the surrounding regions.[50]

But while the horizons of the Antioch community were broadening, the Jerusalem congregation, governed by the Twelve, was increasingly preoccupied with events in the Land of Israel, where another Messiah had appeared.[51] In the year 41, Herod Agrippa, who had been brought up in the imperial household in Rome, had been appointed king of the Upper Jordan Valley by Caligula, the first Jew to hold the royal title since Herod the Great. He was acclaimed joyously by the Jews of Alexandria during his journey eastward, and when he finally arrived in Jerusalem his messianic aura seemed confirmed by more imperial favors: Caligula gave him Galilee and Peraea, the regions formerly ruled by his uncle Antipas, and in gratitude for his support after Caligula's assassination, Claudius made him king of Greater Judea. Agrippa now ruled the whole Land of Israel and had become Rome's most important client in the region.

Agrippa loved and courted his own people, officiating in the temple cult as a scion of King David; in the Mishnah the rabbis would later recall his emotional reading of the Torah at the end of the Feast of Tabernacles. When he came to Moses's description of a truly righteous king — a text widely thought to refer to the Messiah — Agrippa openly wept, hesitating and stumbling over Moses's insistence that this king "be one from among your brothers; you are not to give yourself a foreign king who is no brother of yours."[52] How could he, Agrippa, whose family hailed from Idumea, presume to be the king of Israel? "Do not fear," the crowds shouted, "you *are* our brother!"[53]

But to the followers of Jesus, Agrippa was a false Messiah, and Agrippa launched an attack on their leaders. First he beheaded James, the brother of John, who seems in the very early days to have been second in command to Peter.[54] Then, Luke says, when Agrippa saw that the Jerusalem elite approved of James's execution, he had Peter arrested.[55] Agrippa seemed anxious to gauge Jewish reactions, his chief concern being to retain the loyalty of the priestly aristocracy that had long seen Jesus and his movement as an irritant.[56] But Peter, Luke says, was miraculously delivered from prison and fled the city.[57] He would reappear in Jerusalem later but could no longer govern the community there, and after this incident, we hear no more of the Twelve, who may also have been forced into exile.

The new leader of the Jerusalem assembly was Jesus's brother James, who was able to secure its position in the city. James, known as the Zaddik, the "Just" or "Righteous One," had a special devotion to the temple. The Christian historian Hegesippus (c. 110–c. 180) described him walking around the city clad in linen, like a priest, and performing a special rite in the temple courts that resembled the Yom Kippur ceremony. He "was often found upon his bended knees, interceding for the forgiveness of the people, so that his knees became as calloused as a camel's."[58] Like the Teacher of Righteousness at Qumran, James may have been modeling an alternative priesthood, one that would replace the priestly aristocrats who pandered to imperial rule and had allowed Agrippa to sully the sacred precincts with his messianic affectations.[59]

Agrippa eventually overreached himself and lost favor in Rome. On his last appearance in Caesarea, wearing a dazzling silver coat, he inspired such awe that the crowd cried: "It is a god speaking—not a man!" At once, Luke says, he was struck down for his arrogance and died instantly.[60] Because his son, Agrippa II, was a minor, the kingdom was once again governed by a series of Roman procurators. This resumption of direct Roman rule was a great blow, and James may have concluded that God's Kingdom could be established only by a purified Israel. He may also have wanted to reach out to the Pharisees, who led the opposition to Rome, by his meticulous observance of the Torah, a stance popular with many of Jesus's Jewish followers. Whatever they felt about Jesus, the Torah had an independent authority and mystique, and was sanctioned by centuries of tradition.[61] The ritual laws, which included circumcision and dietary regulations, were not prized merely because Jews wanted to hold aloof from others; rather, they symbolized Israel's priestly service of God in daily life as well as in the cult. First-century Jews knew that their ancestors had preserved their unique identity during their long years in exile in Babylon by living separately, "holy" (*qaddosh*) in the same way as the transcendent God was "set apart." They were acutely aware that the Maccabees had died for these cultic laws in their struggle against the Seleucid king Antiochus Epiphanes (r.175–64 BCE), who had banned circumcision and Sabbath observance. They also knew that Antiochus had been supported by renegade Jews who believed that circumcision was no longer essential. The Maccabees' revolt

(168–143 BCE) had liberated Jews from the Seleucid Empire, and many believed that by faithful observance of the entire Torah, the Jewish people could free themselves of imperial rule yet again. Those gentiles who had made a full conversion to Judaism and undergone the painful ordeal of circumcision were particularly devoted to these special laws; observing them spelled the end of their marginal status and they would have been highly critical of any attempt to disparage them or minimize their importance. Proselytes who joined the Jesus movement brought this attitude with them into the community, convinced that only a truly observant Israel would hasten the Messiah's return.

They may have been among those who, Luke says, arrived in Antioch from Judea toward the end of the 40s CE and "began to teach the brotherhood that those who were not circumcised in accordance with Mosaic practice could not be saved."[62] These newcomers may have found some supporters in Antioch, but Paul and Barnabas opposed them vigorously. For years now, Paul had lived and worked with gentiles and was adamant that the transformative experience of living "in Christ" had nothing to do with the ritual laws of the Torah. He would never reject the Torah; he still saw the ethical commandments as a valuable moral guide for humanity. But he believed that the Messiah's death and resurrection had changed everything and that the Torah had been superseded.[63] Again and again, he had seen that his gentile converts, who had never observed the law, experienced the gifts of the Spirit just like Jesus's Jewish followers. But some Jewish members of the movement regarded him as an apostate. They may have supported a gentile mission but insisted that if pagan converts wanted to belong to the Messiah's community, they must become full Jews. These Judeans regarded Paul's mixed congregations of Jews and gentiles as seriously problematic: Could Jews really live, eat, and marry with gentiles without violating central precepts of the Torah and abandoning centuries of ancestral tradition?

In his letters, Paul never mentioned the visit of these critical Judeans to Antioch. There is nothing to suggest that they had been dispatched by the Jerusalem leadership, since Luke and Paul both made it clear that these conservatives had a different agenda from James, Peter, and John, the "Pillars" of the movement in Judea. They had probably come to the diaspora to investigate these communities on their own initiative, hoping to convince James that, despite Barnabas's earlier report, they were incompatible with Judaism and would, therefore, impede the return of the Messiah and the establishment of the Kingdom.

Luke tells us that Paul and Barnabas had heated discussions with these Judean visitors, and eventually the Antioch leaders commissioned them to lead a delegation to Jerusalem to seek the Pillars' advice. They arrived in the city late in 48 or early in 49 CE.[64] We have two accounts of this meeting. Luke, who may have misunderstood some of the issues, makes it sound as if the Antiochenes were seeking the apostles' approval. But Paul, our only eyewitness, insists in his letter to the Galatians that this was a meeting between equals, a joint struggle to find a reasonable solution to a problem that could divide the movement. Luke, always anxious to assert the authority of the Twelve, describes the Jerusalem summit as an official church council in which the participants delivered formal speeches. At the end, he says, James issued an authoritative statement, known to historians as the Apostolic Decree. Paul, on the other hand, explains that he and his companions simply had "a private interview" with the Pillars: James, Cephas, and John.[65] He had opened the discussion by reporting on the progress of the gentile mission in the hope of convincing the Pillars that the practices of Antioch were truly in line with the ideals of the Jesus movement.[66]

Unfortunately, Paul continues, this informal conversation was interrupted by "certain sham followers of the Messiah, who had sneaked in to spy on the liberty we enjoy in the fellowship of Jesus Christ."[67] Paul and Barnabas had brought Titus, one of their Greek converts, to Jerusalem to show the Pillars that these gentiles were indeed inspired by the same Spirit as Jesus's Jewish followers. Paul, however, knew that Titus's presence would bring matters to a head, and, as he expected, the "intruders" seem to have demanded that Titus be circumcised on the spot. But so compelling was Paul's argument and so authentic was Titus's spirituality that the Pillars ruled against his forcible circumcision and, Paul insists emphatically, they *"did not impose anything further on me."* On the contrary: "They saw that I had been entrusted to take the gospel to the gentiles as surely as Peter had been entrusted to take it to the Jews; for the same God who was at work in Peter's mission to the Jews was also at work in mine to the gentiles."[68] Paul, Barnabas, and the Pillars all shook hands, formally sealing an agreement that had two clauses. First was the acceptance of both Peter's mission to the Jews and Paul's to the gentiles as equally valid—and "nothing further" was demanded in the way of circumcision or ritual observance.[69] The second clause asked that the diaspora communities "should keep in mind the poor," which, Paul says, was "the very thing that I have always made it my business to do."[70]

In years to come, this second stipulation would take on new meaning for Paul, though initially it could simply have been a reminder of the importance of continuing Jesus's original mission to the destitute.[71] But it may also have had a more specific significance. Ever since the time of the Maccabees, Jewish groups that believed that they were the true Israelites—the hidden, oppressed, and persecuted remnant of the End Time—had called themselves "the poor" (*evionim* in Hebrew).[72] The Qumran sectarians and the Jesus community in Jerusalem both styled themselves in this way. The word "poor," therefore, was synonymous with "righteous" or "just"; and James the Zaddik, praying constantly for the sinners of Israel, epitomized the deeply Jewish piety of the *evionim* who lived in the heart of the Holy City.[73] The Pillars, therefore, may have been asking the diaspora assemblies of the movement to remember that they were playing an important role in the eschatological drama that was unfolding, since they would be in Jerusalem to welcome the Messiah when he returned. Paul was eager to do this; he saw Jerusalem as the historic heart of the movement and promised to bring this to the attention of his converts in the gentile world.

But the issues of circumcision and meticulous Torah observance would not go away. Despite the positive outcome of the Jerusalem meeting, Paul's account is bitter and defensive. The "intruders" may have put pressure on James, so that acrimonious debates continued after the Antiochenes left town; as a result of this pressure, it was not long before James did "impose something further" on the gentile followers of Jesus. This addition may be reflected in the Apostolic Decree quoted by Luke, when James had informed all gentile members of the movement: "It is the decision of the Holy Spirit, and our decision, to lay no further burden upon you beyond these essentials: you are to abstain from meat that has been offered to idols, from blood, from anything that has been strangled, and from fornication."[74] This may have been a compromise solution, designed to appease the more conservative Judeans, but it had a fatal flaw. It was based on a ruling in Leviticus that imposed these dietary restrictions not only on Israelites but also on the "stranger" or "foreigner" (*ger*) living among them.[75] Once James had introduced this decree, Paul's critics found a loophole: If the gentile followers of Jesus were merely "strangers" (*gerim*), they were still outsiders and not children of Abraham; if Jews ate the Lord's Supper with these uncircumcised, non-Torah-observant gentiles, they would violate the Torah.

The conflict came to a head in Antioch. Peter was visiting there and at first had taken his meals with the gentile believers; but, Paul says, when "some messengers came from James," he had withdrawn from this table fellowship, in fear of their disapproval. Others followed suit, until at last Paul was the only Jew-

ish member of the Antioch community to remain sitting at the
same table as his gentile brothers and sisters. Even Barnabas, he
would bitterly recall later, "played false like the rest." It was perhaps the most painful rupture of his life, and may explain why
he found it so hard to speak in later years of his time in Antioch. In the presence of the entire community, Paul angrily denounced Peter's defection. In admitting gentiles to the Lord's
Supper, he, Paul, was not doing anything new, he protested. It
was "the truth of the gospel" and this had been affirmed recently
in Jerusalem. It had been the essence of Jesus's message that nobody be excluded from the messianic banquet. It was James who
had shifted the goal posts and betrayed the baptismal affirma-
tion: "No more Jew or Greek!"[76]

Paul believed passionately that the Kingdom would not
come unless the gentiles, filled with the Spirit of God, prayed
for it with their Jewish brothers and sisters in their own way.[77]
Had not God commanded Isaiah: "Let no foreigner who has attached himself to Yahweh say: 'Yahweh will surely exclude me
from his people.'... These I will bring to my holy mountain.
I will make them joyful in my house of prayer, for my house
will be called a house of prayer for all peoples."[78] These were
the words that Jesus had cried when he had chased the money
changers from the temple. Yes, the renewal of Israel to which
James was committed was important, but James had forgotten
God's other charge: "It is not enough for you to restore the cities of Jacob and bring back the survivors of Israel; I will make
you the light of the nations so that my salvation may reach the
ends of the earth."[79]

Soon after the tragic dispute in Antioch there was a parting of ways. Bruised and saddened, feeling perhaps that his mission was in ruins, Paul broke with Barnabas, and together with
Silas, one of the prophets in the Antioch community, he set out
on a mission to "the ends of the earth." He was now convinced
that he alone was true to the gospel, but his Jewish colleagues

may understandably have felt betrayed, because he seemed to be turning his back on the agreement made so affirmatively in Jerusalem. From this point, Paul would become a suspect figure to many in the movement. They would deny his status as an apostle, accuse him of apostasy, and pour scorn on his theology and his manner of preaching. The controversy surrounding Paul would even hasten his death.

3

Land of Japheth

ITHERTO PAUL HAD conducted his mission to the
gentiles in what the Jews called the Land of Shem, fol-
lowing Abraham's legendary tour around the margins of the Promised Land. Now he resolved to cross the Taurus
range and take the gospel to the Land of Japheth, father of the
Greeks, Macedonians, Phrygians, and Anatolians. James and his
supporters probably felt that he was angrily turning his back on
Judaism, but Paul never forgot that he was a Jew. As he made
his way into this alien world, he was accompanied by Silas, an
Aramaic-speaking Jew from Judea, whose presence was a sym-
bolic reminder of the historical roots of the movement. At Lystra, the two were joined by a young man called Timothy, son of
a Jewish woman and a Greek man. Because he was, therefore, legally Jewish, Luke tells us that Paul circumcised him before they
began their journey "out of consideration for the Jews who lived
in those parts."[1] This may or may not be true, but Luke was trying to show that despite the Antioch dispute, Paul was careful to
observe his commitment to respect Peter's mission to the Jews.
Those Jewish followers of Jesus who would later accuse Paul of
instructing diaspora Jews "to break away from Moses, author-
izing them not to circumcise their children or to follow our way
of life" were, Luke implies, incorrect.[2]

The three made no new converts in Lystra, which had already been evangelized by missionaries from Antioch. Paul al-

ways made a point of never preaching in another apostle's territory—a courtesy that his opponents would not observe. Scholars are divided about the route they took on leaving the Taurus region: Some believe that they headed northwest toward the Aegean, but although Paul gives us no information about this journey in his letters, they probably journeyed north to the villages in the Galatian highlands. This was alien territory indeed; unlike Cilicia and Syria, it had few Jewish communities and Jews rarely traveled so far into this wild part of Asia Minor. Paul may initially have been reluctant to seek converts there—Luke says that the Spirit had instructed them not to preach in Asia[3]—but he fell ill and was unable to travel. Later he reminded his Galatian disciples of their great kindness to him: "It was bodily illness, as you will remember, that originally led to my bringing you the gospel, and you resisted any temptation to show scorn or disgust at my physical condition; on the contrary, you welcomed me as if I were an angel of God, as you might have welcomed Christ Jesus himself."[4] When he had sent his disciples into the villages of Galilee, Jesus had told them that when they knocked on a door asking for help and were compassionately taken in, the Kingdom of God had arrived: Paul had direct experience of this in his first venture into the strange Land of Japheth.

We have no idea how Paul instructed his pagan audiences. In his letters, he simply addressed the issues of a particular community, so we have only tantalizing glimpses of his oral preaching. But the epistles suggest that his audience did not always fully understand his message. Communication was difficult because Paul was now speaking to people with entirely different cultural presuppositions and expectations, yet he was nevertheless brilliantly able to adapt the core teachings of the gospel to the traditions and preoccupations of his listeners, and, as he did so, the figure of Jesus gradually altered, taking on a new dimension in each region. The more deeply he entered the gentile world, the more Paul's Christos parted company with the historical Jesus, which had never really interested him in the first place. Far more important to Paul was Jesus's death and resurrection, the cosmic events that had transformed history and changed the fate of all peoples, regardless of their beliefs or ethnicity. If they imitated Jesus's kenosis in their daily behavior, he promised his disciples, they would experience a spiritual resurrection that brought with it a new freedom.[5] The Messiah, he told the Galatians, had given "himself for our sins, to rescue us out of this present wicked age as our God and Father willed."[6]

Paul had experienced his Damascus vision as a liberation from the bondage of the destructive and divisive power of "sin." And freedom seems to have been the theme of his message to the Galatians, who in one sense could not have been more different from the Galilean Jews who had listened to Jesus's teaching. They were an Indo-European people, Aryan Gauls whose native language had been akin to Welsh or Gaelic; in the early third century BCE, they had migrated from Europe and settled in what is now north-central Turkey.[7] An itinerant warrior people, they hired themselves out as mercenaries, before finally adapting to a sedentary lifestyle, living in farming communities ruled by elected assemblies and celebrating the feats of their ancient heroes in rowdy banquets similar to those described in the Anglo-Saxon epic *Beowulf.* They worshipped their Mother Goddess, a fierce deity who enforced justice and was often identified with a mountain that towered above their village; at her major cult centers, young men would sometimes castrate themselves in her orgiastic rituals. What on earth could these savage Celts have in common with Jesus and his Jewish followers?

Yet Paul soon realized that like the Judeans and Galileans, the Galatians had been conquered by Rome relatively recently and were still struggling with imperial rule. Rome had annexed the region in 25 BCE, when it became the province of Galatia, governed by a Roman prefect with a military garrison and a small staff of retainers. Like the Galileans, the Galatians had seen their landscape transformed by the huge agricultural estates owned by absentee landlords that produced the grain that fueled the Roman economy. Gradually their culture too was Romanized; Greco-Roman gods infiltrated their pantheon, and, as loyal subjects, they were required to participate in the imperial cult of the emperor. The agricultural surplus was commandeered by the local aristocracy on Rome's behalf, and as in all agrarian premodern states, these warriors had become little more than serfs, living at subsistence level, their lives controlled by tax collectors and overseers. An intrepid race of heroes now existed for the sole purpose of providing a continuous flow of crops in tax revenue to the imperial capital. As in Galilee and Judea, if they failed to meet the demands of the tribute, they fell into a spiral of debt and were forced either to sell tribal land or to pledge the promise of future harvests. All this would have been very familiar to Paul when he arrived in Galatia, perhaps toward the end of 49 CE; from the letter that he wrote later to the Galatians, we can deduce that he urged them to cast off servile habits of dependence and submission together with the Greco-Roman religion of their masters that supported the imperial order: "Stand firm, therefore, and refuse to submit . . . to the yoke of slavery."[8]

Paul's vision of Christ was rooted in the Jewish apocalyptic tradition that had developed in Israel after the Maccabean wars. Ever since the Seleucid king Antiochus Epiphanes had tried to eradicate *ioudaismos,* scribes, mystics, and poets had developed a mystical spirituality of resistance to imperial culture.[9] The heavenly journeys and visions of cosmic catastrophe experienced by these Jewish mystics were not simply fantasies of wish fulfillment; they were also a shrewd critique of imperial pretension. Most important, they enabled these visionaries to cultivate a conviction that one day they would be free as they meditated intensely on the destruction of their oppressive rulers and the deliverance of Israel. They venerated those martyrs who had died in defense of their sacred traditions and believed that they would either rise from the dead in a collective resurrection or be raised by God to Heaven. Paul the Pharisee was also a visionary, but his Damascus *apocalupsis* differed from the traditional eschatology in two important respects. First, Paul was convinced that in the death of Jesus, God had *already* intervened decisively in history and that the general resurrection had begun when God had raised Jesus from the tomb. Second, Paul believed that God's final deliverance would include the whole of humanity, not Israel alone, so that the ancient promise to Abraham that in him all the nations of the earth would be blessed would be fulfilled.

When Paul came to write his letter to the Galatians, some four years after his visit, he assumed their familiarity with Abraham's story, so it must have figured in his original preaching.[10] But he also drew on terms common in imperial propaganda and turned them upside down. Most striking was his use of *euangelion*, the "good news" or "gospel" that God had announced to the world when he had vindicated Jesus and named him as the Messiah.[11] Throughout the empire, inscriptions, coins, and public rituals announced the "good news" that Augustus, the "savior" (*soter*), had established an era of "peace [*eirene*] and security [*asphaleia*]" throughout the world. But the ubiquitous crosses bearing the tortured bodies of rebels, obscenely torn apart and devoured by birds of prey, were a constant reminder that the Pax Romana was sustained by cruelty and violence. Paul's *euangelion* made the crucified savior a symbol of a fast-approaching liberation from this "present wicked age."

Paul would later recall the spontaneous healings, exorcisms, and glossolalia that had broken out in Galatia as he proclaimed his gospel.[12] The Spirit gave the Galatians the courage to cultivate an ethos of freedom.[13] He would always remember the passionate conviction of their cultic cry after their baptism, when

"God sent the Spirit of his Son into your hearts crying Abba! Father!" The Greek verb *krazein* ("to cry out") suggests an ecstatic, blurting exclamation of joy; when they emerged from the baptismal waters, they were convinced that they were no longer slaves but sons and heirs of the promise that God had made to Abraham.[14]

At the time of Paul's visit, Roman culture was beginning to penetrate the rural areas of Asia Minor. Like colonized people everywhere, the peasants of Galatia would have experienced the sinking loss of identity that comes with enforced acculturation.[15] The Romans believed that they had been appointed by the gods to rule the world and bring civilization to the barbarian peoples, with whom it was impossible to deal on equal terms. This kind of dualism was one of the received ideas of the ancient world, evident also in the Jewish conception of the *goyim* ("the nations") as morally inferior, an attitude that had surfaced so destructively in Antioch. Paul's conviction that the despised "nations" could achieve full equality with Jews challenged fundamental social assumptions.[16] But as they watched the Romanization of their society, some of the Galatians may have been attracted by the prospect of affiliation with Israel, an ethnic group that had won acceptance in the empire, which would enable them to retain some distance from Rome. They not have understood that Paul was insisting on something more radical.[17] He would later remind them in his letter that with the cross the old ethnic, social, and cultural divisions that characterized the present evil age had been obliterated: "Baptized into union with him, you have all put on Christ like a garment. There is no such thing as Jew and Greek, slave and freeman, male or female; for you are all one person in Christ Jesus."[18]

To make the Kingdom a reality, this could not remain an emotional exhilaration but had to be incarnated soberly and practically in daily life. The Galatians had to liberate themselves from habits of servility and ethnic prejudice by creating an alternative community characterized by equality. This community was what Paul meant by life "in Christ." He would call his congregations *ekklesiai* ("assemblies"), regarding them as an implicit challenge to the official *ekklesiai* of local aristocrats that ruled the population of each province as Rome's representatives. The term may also have reminded the Galatians of the elected village assemblies that had ruled their communities before the arrival of the Romans and had taken their responsibility for the welfare of all tribesmen very seriously. Jesus had tried to make God's Kingdom a reality by establishing mutually supportive communities that had made themselves mentally, spiritually, and, to an extent, economically independent of Roman imperium; so too Paul urged the Galatians to create a legal system that united people rather than dividing them into classes and gave equal value to everybody without exception. "The whole law is summed up in a single commandment: love your neighbor as yourself," he urged them.[19] They must transcend the reptilian passions that divided them: "envy, fits of rage, selfish ambitions, dissensions, party intrigues, and jealousies."[20] The law of self-emptying love was "the law of Christ." Where the *ekklesiai* of local aristocrats vaunted their superior status, the Messiah's *ekklesiai* imitated Jesus's kenosis: "If anyone imagines himself to be somebody when he is nothing, he is deluding himself. Each of you should examine his own conduct ... for everyone has his own burdens to bear."[21]

We do not know how long Paul, Silas, and Timothy stayed in Galatia, nor — despite Luke's dramatic story[22] — do we know why they chose Macedonia as their next mission field, arriving in Philippi in the year 50. This too was a very different world for Paul. Founded in 356 BCE by Philip of Macedonia, the city had become the center of the gold-mining industry that had funded the campaigns of Philip's son, Alexander the Great. The mines had long since been exhausted, but Philippi had become the chief Roman outpost on the Via Egnatia, the overland route linking the capital with the eastern provinces. In 42 BCE, after the armies of Mark Antony and Octavian (later known as Augustus) had defeated the coalition of Brutus and Cassius in a battle to the west of the city, Philippi became a Roman colony. Army veterans were settled there and given estates. After the Battle of Actium (31 BCE), which established Augustus as the sole ruler of the empire, more veterans arrived. This was, therefore, a Romanized city with an ethnically mixed population. Yet excavations show that at the time of Paul's visit, Philippi, still a tiny urban enclave comprising only a quarter of a square mile, was merely an administrative center. The bulk of the population lived in farming villages and settlements that served the city in the surrounding countryside. The Roman colonists were exempt from taxation, and they alone could hold political office and were responsible for extracting surplus produce from the villages and landed estates, collecting rents, and enforcing the repayment of loans from indebted peasants.[23]

In Philippi, Paul encountered a particularly intense form of the deification of the Roman emperor. While he was preaching in Macedonia, Claudius, who had sternly forbidden his subjects to build temples in his honor at the beginning of his reign, had begun to promote his cult in the provinces and, like Augustus, had assumed the title "savior of the world." Scholars have sometimes dismissed the emperor cult as "purely secular," a political strategy with no "religious" content that was exploited by the Roman state and local aristocracies for their own purposes.[24] But in Paul's time, religion and political life were so intertwined that it was impossible to say where one began and the other ended. The followers of Jesus were not the only ones to proclaim the "good news" that a new age was dawning. "A great new cycle of centuries begins!" the poet Virgil exclaimed. "Justice returns to earth, the golden age returns."[25] In Priene, on the coast of modern Turkey, an inscription announced that the birthday of "the most divine Caesar [Augustus]" marked the beginning of a new era and a new calendar. It was a date "which we might justly set on a par with the beginning of everything, in practical terms at least, in the restored order, when everything was disintegrating and falling into chaos, and gave a new look to the whole world." Indeed, Caesar had "exceeded the hopes of those who prophesied good tidings [*euaggelia*]."[26] Throughout the empire, temples, coins, and inscriptions hailed each successive Caesar as "son of god," "god made manifest," "lord," and "savior of the world."[27]

These claims were more credible in the ancient world than they would be today, since no vast ontological gulf separated the human from the divine: Men and women regularly became gods and vice versa. Studies have shown that the sacrifices to the emperor's *genius* ("divine spirit") were not empty rituals but the means by which the subject peoples conceptualized the power that now ruled the known world, helping them to make sense of the intrusion of Rome into their lives by drawing on familiar imagery and concepts of kingship.[28] In bringing peace and security to a world ravaged by incessant warfare, Augustus seemed to have performed a divine task that was not unlike the Olympian gods' ordering of the cosmos. Most significantly, the cult was not forced on the provinces by the Roman Senate but was enthusiastically embraced by the local aristocracies. They actually vied with one another in building temples and shrines to the reigning emperor and erecting inscriptions praising his achievements. So did the wealthy freedmen, who used the cult to gain recognition and status. In Hellenistic society, the elite were obsessed with *philotimia,* the love of public honor, which they courted by making gifts of buildings, shrines, and inscriptions to be prominently displayed in their city. Promoting the emperor cult was one of the best ways of winning Rome's favor, so aristocrats strove to outdo one another in their devotion to the cult. Imperial rituals saturated every aspect of public life in the provinces, invading public space in rather the same way as the sights and sounds of Christmas in modern Western countries. Aristocrats not only paid for these sacrifices but also officiated in the emperor cult as priests, the highest status symbol of all. The cult gained such wide acceptance that by the end of Augustus's reign, to attribute "divine honors" (*isotheoi timai*) to anyone but the emperor had become politically undesirable.[29]

Emperor worship was far more prominent in the Land of Japheth than in Syria and Cilicia, so it would have made a painful impression on Paul, not simply because it was religiously offensive but because of its political and social implications. Macedonia and Achaea had been conquered originally by military force, but, unlike Judea and Galatia, these provinces were now so completely pacified that there was no need for Rome to establish a military presence there and the capital could rely on the loyalty of the local ruling class. Instead, the imperial cult acted as the glue that pulled its vast empire together in allegiance to Rome, backed by a tight network of patronage relationships.[30]

When Augustus had become the sole ruler of the empire, he had called for a return to traditional Roman values, especially *pietas*, duty to family and country. He presented himself to the citizens of Rome as their father and patron, manifesting his paternal devotion in massive public benefactions. In return, he expected his subjects' loyalty (*pistis*). In the provinces too, the local elite depicted their emperor as the benevolent bringer of peace and security whose rule was blessed by the gods, so the conquered peoples were expected to love their subjugation. But Paul would soon have become aware of the structural injustice of the Roman system, which created an unbridgeable social chasm between the aristocratic ruling class and the common people. Rich and poor dressed differently, they ate different food, and spoke virtually different languages. The masses were expected to show their deference to their superiors in myriad stylized rituals in the course of a single day. And the ubiquitous spectacle of the cross was a reminder of what could happen if you stepped out of line and laid bare the cruelty on which this supposedly benign system depended.

Because, as a Roman colony, Philippi followed the customs of Rome and Italy, the emperor cult there may have been particularly intense. In later years, when Paul wrote to the Philippian congregation, he quoted the Christ Hymn, which described Jesus's kenosis and subsequent exaltation by God. In this environment, where it was an offense to accord "divine honors" to anybody but the emperor, chanting this hymn could have dangerous consequences.[31] The hymn stated clearly that unlike the emperor, who *did* seek "equality with god" (*isa theo*), Jesus had not tried to "grasp" this distinction himself; his elevation to the divine realm had been entirely God's initiative to reward Jesus for his humble acceptance of death on a Roman cross. Paul's converts in Philippi, of course, came from the poorer classes of society and did not have the same rights as Roman citizens. But Paul told them to declare de facto independence of the imperial system. Philippi might be a Roman colony, but their *ekklesia* was a "colony of heaven." A colony shares the ethos of the mother country rather than that of the indigenous culture, so they were citizens of Heaven, their true commonwealth (*politeuma*), and their "savior" was not Claudius but Jesus the Messiah.[32] They would make this a reality by creating a mutually supportive community. Instead of engaging in the tireless self-promotion of the elite, they must imitate the kenosis of Jesus. "Leave no room for selfish ambition or vanity, but humbly reckon others better than yourselves. Look to each other's interests and not merely your own."[33] This would enable them to stand firm in the face of harassment from the authorities in this "crooked and depraved generation," shining "like stars in a dark world."[34]

These social bonds were reinforced by signs of emergent organization. Paul was creating a network of "coworkers" to help him draw his far-flung communities together. In Philippi, they included Clement and Epaphroditas and two women, Synteche and Euodia. In Paul's congregations there seem to have been roughly as many male as female leaders, since "in Christ" gender equality, as well as class and ethnic equity, was mandatory. When he wrote to the Philippian *ekklesia*, he breached Greco-Roman conventions by deliberately drawing attention to these women, noting that they had "shared my struggles in the cause of the gospel."[35] The Philippians would become Paul's most faithful disciples: Before he left the city, they made a financial commitment out of their own meager resources to support his mission.[36]

Paul's subversive teaching may have caused his expulsion from the city; he would write of the "injury and outrage" that he and his companions had suffered in Philippi. But undeterred, he pressed on, penetrating still more deeply into the world of Roman dominance, until he arrived in Thessalonica. Since 146 BCE, the city had been the capital of the province of Macedonia and the emperor cult was strong there. The Thessalonian aristocrats honored their powerful Roman patrons alongside their own gods in inscriptions, public oratory, and festivals.[37] During the first century BCE, the goddess Roma had been added to the local pantheon, with her own priesthood, and a temple was built for Augustus. At the same time, Julius Caesar replaced Zeus on the city coinage, and though Augustus was not explicitly titled "son of God" in Thessalonica, as Julius Caesar's adopted son, he was implicitly acknowledged as *divi filius,* son of the divine Julius.[38]

Paul introduced the Thessalonians to a new "lord" (*kyrios*), "son of God" (*theou huios*), and "savior" (*soter*). Other redeemer gods were popular in the city, notably Cabirus, a blacksmith murdered by his brothers who would one day return to help the poor and needy. But the aristocracy had co-opted Cabirus into their own rituals, and Paul could present Jesus as a more authentic savior.[39] He would long remember the enthusiasm with which the Thessalonians had welcomed the gospel, because it became famous in the Jesus movement: "Everyone is spreading the story of our visit to you," he would write to them later, "how you turned from idols to be servants of the true and living God, and to wait expectantly for his Son from heaven . . ."[40] Here too Paul founded an *ekklesia* that was a direct challenge to the citizens' assembly of the elite, since it comprised artisans and laborers in the lower echelons of the stratified urban economy.[41] Paul told them to honor their own leaders, who were "working so hard among you," rather than the ruling class.[42] Solidarity and mutual support rather than social inequity must characterize the Messiah's *ekklesia*.[43] He himself worked side by side with other artisans in his workshop, where he preached the gospel, and would later remember the "toil and drudgery" of this time as he labored at his trade "night and day . . . rather than be a burden to any of you"— an existence very different from Luke's account of Paul engaging in important public debates in the synagogues of Thessalonica.[44]

Here too Paul encountered overt hostility, and would recall how he, Silas, and Timothy had preached "frankly and fearlessly in the face of great opposition." He had warned the Thessalonians that they too would probably suffer for the sake of the gospel.[45] Claudius had recently expelled from Rome Jews who may have been members of the Jesus movement, because, the historian Suetonius explained, they were agitating in the name of one "Chrestus." But Paul was not in favor of such overt action. Instead, the Thessalonians should wait peaceably for Jesus's return. In this interim period, he told them, "live quietly and attend to your own business . . . so that you may command the respect of those outside your own numbers."[46] Yes, they were indeed the children of light grappling with the forces of darkness, but they were armed only with spiritual weapons: "the breastplate of faith and love, and the hope of salvation for a helmet."[47]

Before long Paul had to leave Thessalonica in a hurry. Luke, as usual, lays the blame on the local Jewish community, who complained to the local magistrates that Paul and Silas had turned the world upside down with their teaching: "All of them flout the emperor's laws, and assert that there is a rival king, Jesus."[48] Luke may have captured the subversive tenor of Paul's teaching here. Undeterred, Paul journeyed westward. From his letters we learn that he spent some time alone in Athens, sending Timothy back to Thessalonica to see how the community was faring. Luke's account of Paul's visit has become famous. He describes Paul preaching before the Council of the Areopagus like a Greek philosopher, arguing from the evidence of natural reason for the existence of a God, praised by Greek poets as "not far from each one of us, for in him we live and move, in him we exist."[49] Paul had little time for Greek wisdom, however, and it is more likely that Luke was describing what he himself would have said had he had the good luck to speak in Athens, even though by this time its golden age was long past. There is no historical evidence that Paul made any converts or founded a community there.

Paul was more interested in the modern cities of the empire, and in the autumn of 50 CE, he arrived in Corinth, the most prosperous city of Achaea. The ancient *polis* had resisted Roman expansion in 146 BCE and had been totally destroyed, lying in ruins for over a century as a stark reminder of the price of opposition to Rome. In 44 BCE, Julius Caesar had rebuilt and repopulated Corinth with freed slaves, and under Augustus it became the capital of the province of Achaea, with a proconsul as governor. By the time Paul arrived, it ranked as the fourth most important city in the empire. Situated on the isthmus linking northern and southern Greece, it was a thriving trading hub with a mixed community of conscripted freedmen from Italy, Greece, Syria, Egypt, and Judea. It was ruled by an aristocracy of uprooted but ambitious self-made men, who wanted to forget their lowly origins and enjoy the wealth of the city. But Paul would have noticed the glaring disparity between their opulent neighborhoods and the crowded workshops and impoverished industrial quarters where he and his disciples lived. In Corinth, he became even more aware of the structural violence of the Roman patronage system, in which the local ruling class dominated all lines of communication with Rome and controlled the scarce resources of wealth, power, and prestige. Acquiring a powerful patron, either at home or in Rome, was the only route to advancement.

Like the imperial cult, the patronage system bound the Roman Empire together. A patron would collect clients to boost his own status with his peers; he would promise to help these dependents, but his power lay in his ability to refuse or delay such assistance, keeping his clients dependent and in suspense. Because most of the poor were tied in this way to the wealthy families, the system thus became an instrument of social control that was contingent on its inequity. As one historian explains, "The inability of a few hundred to satisfy the needs of hundreds of thousands, their manifest failure to alleviate poverty, hunger and debt, indeed their exploitation of those circumstances to secure themselves advantage need not be seen as arguments for the inadequacy of patronage, so much as the conditions of its flourishing."[50]

In their turn, local aristocrats in the provinces relied on the patronage of powerful men in the imperial capital. These Roman patrons expressed their loyalty (*pistis*) to the provinces by helping their "friends" there; in return, these "friends" were rewarded for their *pistis* to Rome. Roman governors in the provinces also depended on the patronage of their "friends" in the capital and ruled by building a local power base, cultivating a loyal clientele of "friends" among the local nobility. They all vied with one another to display their loyalty to the emperor by participating enthusiastically in his cult. There was no pretense of parity in these friendships, since accepting clientage was itself a tacit admission of inferiority. Lesser aristocrats and freedmen competed with one another by building their own networks of loyal clients from the lower classes. As the Roman senator and historian Tacitus explained, the "good" people in a city were defined by their attachment and *pistis* to the great families, while the "bad" took no part in the patronage system, either because they had nothing to offer the rich or because they deliberately avoided this humiliating subordination.[51]

Paul cast himself as one of the "bad" people in Corinth by persistently refusing to accept any financial support from local patrons. Instead, he continued to work as an artisan, lodging with a Jewish couple, Aquila and Prisca, who were also tentmakers. They had been among the Jews expelled from Rome by Claudius and became loyal friends and colleagues of Paul's.[52] In Corinth, Paul conducted his mission in their workshop, preaching while he worked, and yet again the gospel was received by an outpouring of the Spirit as his converts found themselves able to prophesy, speak in tongues, and heal the sick.[53] Small congregations developed in the private households of the artisans and shopkeepers who assembled around Paul's bench. Yet again, it was the poor who accepted the gospel. God, Paul told the Corinthians, had "chosen things without rank or standing in the world, mere nothings, to overthrow the existing order."[54] By executing the Messiah, the powers that be had condemned themselves to destruction. The Messiah was now enthroned at the right hand of God, preparing to depose "every sovereignty, authority, and power."[55] In Corinth, the cross was central to Paul's message. When he had raised Jesus, the disgraced criminal, from the dead, God had displayed his *pistis* to the despised of this world. Where the emperor cult deified power and wealth, the cross had revealed an entirely new set of divine values.

Paul would share his metaphor of the body of Christ with his Corinthian congregation, a vision that overturned the official imperial theology in which the body was the microcosm of both the state and the cosmos.[56] Caesar was the head of the body politic; he personified the earthly state and represented the gods in the heavenly world. But there was no such hierarchy in the body of the Messiah. Instead, Paul described an interrelated order in which all members, without exception, depended upon one another. The head was demoted and the inferior body parts elevated. Paul expressed this important political insight with the kind of risqué humor used by orators to startle their audience into a new perspective.

> It is precisely the parts of the body that seem to be the weakest which are the indispensable ones, and it is the least honorable parts of the body that we clothe with the greatest care. So our more improper parts get decorated in a way that our more proper parts do not need. God has arranged the body so that more dignity is given to the humbler parts, so that there might not be disagreements inside the body but that each part may be equally concerned for all the others. If one part is hurt, all parts are hurt with it. If one part is given special honor, all parts enjoy it.[57]

Paul stayed in Corinth for eighteen months, but toward the end of his visit, in the spring of 52 CE, there was disturbing news from Thessalonica. Apparently the community there had suffered some kind of persecution, but Paul had been overjoyed to hear Timothy's glowing report of their fidelity and perseverance under trial. Now, however, the Thessalonian leaders wrote to Paul in some perplexity. He had promised that they would all see the Lord's glorious return but, possibly as a result of the recent harassment, some of the community had died. Would they also join the Messiah's triumph? Yes, Paul replied emphatically in the first of his letters to have survived.

While living in the gentile world, Paul's imagination had been saturated by the Roman symbolism that permeated the atmosphere in which he and his converts and coworkers thought and felt. Imperial propaganda constantly vaunted the "peace" (*eirene*) and "security" (*asphaleia*) that Rome had brought to the world, but this, Paul suggested to the Thessalonians, was a delusion that the Messiah's coming would shatter: "While they are saying, 'All is peaceful, all secure,' destruction is upon them, sudden as the pangs that come on a woman in childbirth; and there will be no escape."[58] When he described the dramatic arrival of the Christ, instead of drawing on the conventional imagery of Jewish apocalypse, he used terminology that was quite new to the Jesus movement, presenting Jesus's return as an official visit of an emperor or king to a provincial city.

> When the command is given, when the archangel's voice is heard, when God's trumpet sounds, then the Lord himself will descend from heaven; first the dead who belong to the Messiah will arise, then we who are still alive shall join them, caught up in the clouds to meet the Lord in the air.[59]

The word *parousia* ("presence"), which referred to the ceremonial "arrival" of the visiting emperor, recurs throughout the letter.[60] As soon as the officials heard that the emperor was actually approaching the city, the trumpet would sound and a delegation of local dignitaries would pour through the city gates and surge toward him for the ritualized *apantesis* ("meeting").[61] In Paul's description, of course, Jesus, the true Kyrios, has replaced Claudius and the people who throng to meet him are Paul's converts, who are no longer the weak and oppressed inhabitants of the city but its most privileged citizens. They will go up in the air to greet their Lord and bring him down to earth. In the person of Jesus, his representative, God would, as it were, leave the heavenly realm and join the common people.[62]

In the summer of 52 CE, Paul finally left Corinth and sailed to Ephesus. If, as Luke claims, Lucius Junius Gallio became the

governor of Corinth while Paul was in residence, his stay co-
incided with a more assertive Roman presence in the city and
thus Paul became persona non grata.[63] He was accompanied by
Aquila and Prisca, who settled in the city; Ephesus would become his home for two and a half years. There he was joined
by Titus, his old friend from Antioch, who took the gospel to
the surrounding districts. Briefly present also in Ephesus was an
eloquent and charismatic Alexandrian Jew called Apollos, who
would cause Paul a great deal of trouble.[64] A new and distressing
chapter in his life was about to begin.

4

Opposition

THE TROUBLE BEGAN with worrying news from the Galatian highlands; it seems that Paul's converts there had met some Jewish members of the Jesus movement who claimed that he was a false teacher. Paul, they said, had no right to tell them that they were children of Abraham; they could earn that privilege only if they were circumcised and observed the Law of Moses. Paul was horrified; yet again, the issue that had erupted so painfully in Antioch threatened his entire mission. He had always maintained that it was unnecessary for gentiles who committed themselves to the Messiah to observe the Torah, since they had received the Spirit without its help. The Torah was valuable to Jews, but it could only be a distraction to the Galatians; forcing them to adopt a wholly Jewish way of life would be as absurd as demanding that Jews take on the ancient Galatian traditions and start feasting like Aryan warriors, singing their drinking choruses, and venerating their warrior heroes.[1] He fired off a letter to the Galatian *ekklesia*, urging its members in the strongest terms to reject this advice. Had they not declared after their baptism that the old distinctions of race, class, and gender were irrelevant in the community of the Christ that they had created? They must at all costs retain the freedom they had experienced with such joy.

Who were the people who, as Paul saw it, were leading the Galatians astray? They have often been identified with the "in-

truders" who had interrupted Paul's conference with the Pillars
in Jerusalem or the "messengers from James" who had caused
such ferment in Antioch. But it seems more likely that instead
of being envoys from Judea, they were local people, evangelized
by Jewish missionaries of the Jesus movement who did not share
Paul's views. Like James, they believed that fidelity to the Torah was essential for the renewal of Israel that would accelerate
the Messiah's return. Because some of the Galatians may have
thought that joining Israel would be preferable to acculturation
in the Roman ethos, they would have been extremely distressed
to hear that their status was in fact ambiguous and that they
were neither one thing nor the other. In Roman law, Jews were
officially exempt from the emperor cult because an offering was
made daily for the reigning emperor in the Jerusalem temple.
Once they had become full members of Israel, as they believed,
the Galatians had enjoyed this exemption. But now that they
were no longer bona fide Jews, they would be liable to harassment or even persecution by the authorities if they refused to
take part in the imperial cult, which had become repugnant to
them since they renounced paganism.[2] Some of the Galatians
had decided to become proselytes and had already embarked on
the process of conversion to Judaism, but Paul vehemently insisted that this was unnecessary.[3]

The incident reminds us that at this early phase, Paul's was
only one voice among many others. His ideas would later become normative in Christianity, so we tend to see his firm stand
against circumcision and observance of Jewish ritual law as un-
avoidable. Had he not done so, we assume, Christianity would
have dwindled to an insignificant Jewish sect, since very few
gentiles would have been willing to undergo the dangerous op-
eration of circumcision. Paul's opponents in Galatia are seen as
aggressive "Judaizers," trapped in what Christians have termed
the chronic "legalism" of Judaism, an attitude that has gravely
damaged Christian-Jewish relations. In fact, Paul's uncompro-

mising stance on this issue was not typical. As a Pharisee, Paul had believed that once a person had been circumcised, he had to observe the entire Torah, including the mass of orally transmitted legal traditions of Israel that would later be codified in the Mishnah.[4] But not many other Jews would have agreed with Paul, and the rabbis would eventually decide that circumcision was not necessary for salvation since "there are righteous men among the gentiles who have a share in the world to come."[5] As far as we know, no other Jewish missionaries in the Jesus movement took Paul's hard line. Apart from his letters, all the New Testament scriptures were written for Jewish communities that included gentiles, which seemed untouched by Paul's ideas. Far from finding the Jewish ritual laws burdensome, a significant number of gentiles seem to have found them attractive and Pauline converts seemed not only willing but actually eager to take them on.[6]

Paul's opponents in Galatia believed that Jesus's heroic death and resurrection had inspired a spiritual renewal movement within Israel; they advocated continuity with the past. But Paul believed that with the cross something entirely new had come into the world.[7] By raising Jesus, a criminal condemned by Roman law, God had taken the shocking step of embracing what the Torah deemed defiled. Jewish law decreed: "Cursed is everyone who is hanged on a gibbet"; by accepting this shameful death, Jesus had made himself legally profane, voluntarily becoming an abomination. But by raising him to the highest place in Heaven, God had vindicated Jesus, cleared him of all guilt, and in the process declared Roman law null and void and the Torah's categories of purity and impurity no longer valid. As a result, gentiles, hitherto ritually unclean, could also inherit the blessings promised to Abraham without becoming subject to Jewish law.

Unlike his opponents, Paul stressed discontinuity, but in doing so he violated some of the most fundamental values of his time. In the ancient world, originality was not prized as it is today. Our modern economy has enabled us to institution-alize change in a way that was previously impossible. An agrar-ian economy simply could not develop beyond a certain limit and was unable to afford the constant replication of the infra-structure that we take for granted today. People experienced civ-ilization as fragile and preferred to put their trust in traditions that had stood the test of time. The great antiquity of Judaism had won the respect of Rome, but Romans regarded new forms of religious expression as *superstitio,* an object of dread, because they lacked reverence for ancestral tradition. So instead of find-ing Paul's vision exciting, many of the Galatians would have been gravely disturbed to hear that most Jews saw their position as an impious breach with the past.

Paul understood all this perfectly. He knew that he was asking the Galatians to question attitudes and principles that seemed cast in stone. In his letter, therefore, he wrote in the rhe-torical form known as the diatribe. Rhetoric, the art of persua-sive language, was the core subject of the Greco-Roman cur-riculum; boys were trained to write and speak in a style that would influence their audiences and persuade them to take a particular course of action. The diatribe was designed in such a way as to force an audience to call fundamental presuppo-sitions into question. When we read Paul's letters it is impor-tant to understand that at this time letters were not perused si-lently. Instead, they were read aloud, with gestures, mime, and visual aids, to drive a point home. An epistle, therefore, was es-sentially a speech act and a dramatic performance.[8] When Paul had preached his doctrine of the cross to the Galatians during his visit, he may have brought home the extremity of this event by showing them a graphic painting of the crucified Christ — or even stood beneath a cross, pointing to the tortured body of a man crucified by the authorities in one of their villages. So in his letter, he berated them: "You stupid Galatians! You must have been bewitched — you before whose eyes Jesus Christ was openly displayed on the cross!"⁹

To a modern reader, Paul's aggressive style in this letter seems insulting and personally offensive. But in the first century, even an unlettered audience would have recognized that this was a convention; Paul was writing in a literary form in which exaggeration, mockery, and even insults were expected. When he attacked Jewish law in this diatribe, he was not claiming that Judaism was wrong per se, nor was he drawing on his own experience. As we have seen, Paul the Pharisee had had no problem with Torah observance; indeed, he was convinced that he had excelled in his fulfilment of the law. In his letters, he was not writing for Everyman and never intended to make a general ruling applicable to everybody, but was always addressing a specific problem in a particular congregation. Nor was he legislating for future generations of Christians, since he expected the Parousia in his own lifetime. In this letter, he was speaking very precisely to the unique predicament of his Galatians, telling them what he believed was right for *them* — not for the human race as a whole. Nor was he denigrating the Jewish people in this letter. He was simply arguing with his Jewish opponents, who, he believed, did not have the Galatians' best interests at heart.

He began, as we have seen, by telling his own story — the Damascus revelation, his relationship with Peter and James, the Jerusalem Conference, and, finally, the bitter parting of the ways in Antioch. His purpose was to explain to the Galatians that he was not surprised about what had occurred because something similar had happened to him, not once but twice: first, when the "intruders" had interrupted his conversation with the Pillars, and second, when the "messengers from James" had arrived in Antioch. He was also anxious to point out that at the Jerusalem summit, James and Peter had affirmed his Torah-free mission to the gentiles, because the authenticity of Titus's faith had convinced them that gentiles could be "justified" (*dikaiousthai*) — or made right with God — by the faith of Jesus the Messiah, so that there was no need for them to submit to circumcision or the ritual laws of the Torah.[10] Later, of course, James and even Peter had reneged on that agreement.

Before the twentieth century, the phrase *pistis Iesou Christou* was regularly translated into English as "the faith or loyalty *of* Jesus." It did not refer to the faith of ordinary mortals, but only to the "trust" that Jesus had in God when he accepted his death sentence and his "confidence" that God would turn it to good; and God had indeed rewarded this act of faith by inaugurating a new relationship with humanity that saved men and women from the iniquity and injustice of the old order, ensuring that all people, whatever their social status or ethnicity, could become God's children. But ever since the publication of the American Standard Version of the Bible in 1901, this phrase has regularly been translated as "faith *in* Jesus Christ," equated with an individual Christian's *belief* in Jesus's divinity and redemptive act.[11]

Paul went on to argue that the Torah had not been revealed for all time but had been only a temporary arrangement. He illustrated his point by comparing the Jewish people with an heir to a great estate: As long as the boy is a minor, he has no more freedom of action than a slave; he is emancipated and enjoys the privileges of a son only when he reaches his majority. So it was with us Jews, Paul explained to the Galatians. But then God sent his son "to buy freedom for those who were under the law in order that we might achieve the status of sons."[12] For Jews like himself, he explained, the law had fulfilled the function of a *paidogogus,* the slave who accompanied children to school, ensuring that they behaved themselves and came to no harm until he had delivered them safely to their teacher, when their true education began. "The law was thus put in charge of us until the Messiah should come," Paul continued, "and now that faith has come, its charge is at an end."[13] It was because of the faith that Jesus had shown on the cross, Paul told the Galatians, "that you are all sons of God in union with Jesus Christ"; Jews and gentiles were now in the same boat, since the old divisions and categories no longer applied.[14]

The German scholar Dieter Georgi, however, has argued that Paul was not simply speaking of the Torah in this letter but was referring to law in general. In the diaspora, the universalizing outlook of some Hellenized Jews had led them, like some of the Greek philosophers, to regard the ancestral laws of various peoples as different reflections of the will of God. So they maintained that Israel was not alone in possessing God's law; each nation had developed its own version of the eternal law that exists in the mind of God. Greeks and Romans certainly believed that their legal systems were divinely ordained, just as Jews did, but ever since Damascus, Paul had developed a more jaundiced view of law. The emperors claimed that Roman law brought "justice" (*dikaiosune*), yet it had condemned Jesus to death. When Paul heard the word *dikaiosune,* he immediately interpreted it in the light of the Greek translation of the Hebrew Bible.[15] For the prophets, justice had meant social equality; they had denounced rulers who failed to treat the pauper, the widow, and the foreigner with equity and respect. From what Paul had seen in his travels, Roman law had failed to implement justice in this sense; it favored only the privileged few and had virtually enslaved the vast majority of the population.

In his letter to the Thessalonians, Paul had depicted God declaring his solidarity with those whom Roman law ignored. When God had exalted Jesus to his right hand, he had allied himself with the victims of oppression. To the Galatians, he presented Jesus as voluntarily subjecting himself to the law's condemnation and demonstrating his solidarity with the most abject members of the human race. The social unity, democracy, egalitarianism, and freedom extolled in Hellenistic ideology could not be achieved by any form of jurisprudence, because, despite its lofty idealism, in practice law always enslaved, denigrated, and destroyed. The legal systems of the world had divided Romans from barbarians and Jews from gentiles; they privileged men over women; they created aristocrats who lorded it over slaves. In Antioch, the strict adherence to law had meant that Jews and gentiles were unable to eat at the same table. If the baptismal cry—"There is no such thing as Jew and Greek, slave and freeman, male and female, for you are one person in Christ Jesus"—were to become a social reality, there would have to be a fundamental reevaluation of the notion of authority and what was really sacred.[16]

No sooner had Paul dispatched his letter to Galatia than there was news of serious trouble in Corinth. A delegation of "Chloe's people"—probably members of Chloe's household congregation in Corinth—had arrived in Ephesus to tell him that the Corinthian *ekklesia* had split up into acrimonious factions. The Alexandrian Jew Apollos, whom Paul may have met in Ephesus, was preaching a "spiritualized" form of the gospel, which gave those who embraced it a superior "wisdom", which, they claimed, had elevated them to a higher plane than ordinary mortals. Peter, it seems, had also arrived in Corinth with a different message from Paul's, and because he had actually known Jesus, he was also attracting disciples. Finally, upwardly mobile Corinthians were trying to boost their social position in the city by acting as patrons to some of the household congregations and were providing the food for the Lord's Supper. These new members had no time for Paul's egalitarian gospel; they were drawing the movement into the patronage network that depended and thrived on inequity. Vying with one another for power and prestige, patrons and clients alike were actually treating the gifts of the Spirit as status symbols.[17]

Who was Apollos and what was he preaching? Luke tells us that he was full of spiritual fervor and that he taught the facts about Jesus's life and death accurately, but that "the only baptism he knew was John's."[18] John the Baptist had featured prominently in Q, the earliest gospel, which may have been committed to writing at about this time. Apollos could have heard stories about John and Jesus during a pilgrimage to Jerusalem. He would have heard the story of Jesus's baptism, when the Spirit had descended on him and a divine voice proclaimed, "This is my beloved Son, in whom I take delight."[19] Paul believed that Jesus had become God's son only when he was raised from the dead, but Apollos and his followers thought that this had happened at his baptism.[20] Who could say who was right? Apollos believed that when Jesus's followers were baptized, they too became "sons of God," that is, perfected and wholly fulfilled human beings in whom God delighted.[21] Apollos taught that the human being consisted of flesh (*sarx*), soul (*psyche*), and spirit (*pneuma*) and that these different aspects were constantly at war with one another.[22] But after baptism, the Spirit reigned supreme in the new Christian, manifesting its presence in the gifts of prophecy, healing, and speaking in tongues. His disciples in Corinth, the *pneumatikoi* ("spirituals"), believed that the Kingdom had already come in its fullness and that they had already gained immortality; they were not waiting eagerly for the Parousia, because they had already attained the highest human state possible, as their visions, revelations, and prophecies proved.[23] In fact, they formed a "spiritual aristocracy."

Apollos had been influenced by the Jewish Wisdom tradition that had been preached originally by the Jewish philosopher Philo of Alexandria. It was based on a personal devotion to Sophia, "Divine Wisdom," an attribute or emanation of God.[24] This spirituality had enabled Jews who felt humiliated by living under imperial rule to recover a sense of dignity, because they had achieved a wisdom that was superior to that of their rulers.[25] Thanks to Apollos, the despised artisans and laborers of Corinth had become intoxicated by similar fantasies, believing that because they were perfected human beings, they could now claim a noble lineage, worldly honor, and social distinction without being corrupted by these worldly attainments.[26]

This was exhilarating stuff for artisans, slaves, and shopkeepers and opened up all kinds of exciting possibilities. Because they thought they had achieved a higher spiritual knowledge, the *pneumatikoi* were no longer bound by rules and conventions that were obligatory for the "unspiritual person."[27] They had already achieved the liberty of the sons of God, so they could say, "All things are possible for me."[28] Those eager to climb the social ladder felt free to attend the public sacrifices and banquets (without which it was impossible to advance in society) and eat the flesh of sacrificial victims, because they knew that the idols worshipped in these rituals did not exist.[29] Thanks to the Spirit, they now had full control over their bodies, and women were leaving their husbands and opting for the freedom of celibacy; other "spirituals" were even contracting marriages that were incestuous but socially advantageous and sleeping with prostitutes.[30] Still others were aggressively pursuing their own interests by suing other members of the Jesus movement in the pagan courts.[31]

Paul, needless to say, found all this abhorrent. In a long letter, he answered the questions put to him by "Chloe's people," taking the argument that he had begun in his letter to the Galatians a step further. He started by reminding the Corinthians that during his stay, the focus of his preaching had been the crucified Christ. He now applied this to the teaching of the *pneumatikoi*. Jewish Wisdom writers described Sophia as the "flawless mirror of the active power of God" and "an undefiled radiance, making all things new." She was "more beautiful than the sun, and surpasses every constellation," and "She spans the world in power from end to end, and gently orders all things."[32] But Paul shattered this limpid myth of purity, power, gentleness, and beauty by evoking the horrifying image of the cross. When God had raised the body of a convicted criminal to his right hand, he had "made the wisdom of this world seem foolish."[33] While Jews saw the cross as a scandal and for Greeks it could only be folly, the "Christ nailed to a cross" had been a new revelation of what "the power and wisdom of God" really meant.[34] Conventional ideas of the divine and of human achievement had been turned upside down.

In this scenario, there could be "no place left for any human pride" and no basis for the preposterous claims made by the "spirituals." Instead, Paul mercilessly cut them down to size, reminding them that in reality "Few of you are wise by any human standard, few powerful or of noble birth." When the Messiah's community confessed Jesus as God's decisive revelation to the world, they were preaching a wisdom that the world could not understand. Had the Romans understood it, "they would not have crucified the Lord of glory."[35] The cross had overturned all forms of power, dominance, and authority, showing that the divine manifested itself not in strength but in weakness.

Paul then began to answer the questions put to him by Chloe's people; in each case, the basis of his argument was the importance of community. To live "in Christ" was not a private affair; as he had always insisted, it was achieved when people put the needs of others before their own and lived together in love. Instead of exalting themselves as a spiritual aristocracy, the true followers of Jesus imitated his kenosis. As the Christ Hymn had pointed out, Jesus had achieved his high status only by emptying himself and accepting death on a cross. It was in this letter to the Corinthians that Paul developed the image of the body of Christ, a community that was interdependent and pluralistic and honored what the world regarded as base. He was horrified by the factions that were tearing this "body" apart: "Each of you is saying, 'I am for Paul,' or 'I am for Apollos'; 'I am for Cephas,' and 'I am for Christ.' Surely Christ has not been divided!"[36]

Because faith in Christ was not a private quest but an experiment in living together, Paul passionately opposed the individualism promoted by the "spirituals," urging them instead to focus on the unity and integrity of the whole *ekklesia*. He was disgusted to hear that members of the Messiah's congregation were taking out lawsuits against one another.[37] When the "spirituals" claimed that they were free to have sex with prostitutes, they violated the sacred reality of this community: "Do you not know that your bodies are limbs and organs of Christ? Shall I then take parts of Christ's body and make them over to a prostitute?"[38] The man who had married his stepmother to cement his links with the nobility was polluting the whole community, just as yeast leavens an entire batch of bread.[39] Given the sexual immorality for which Corinth was famous, those women who were leaving their husbands and those unmarried men who were refusing to take wives were asking for trouble.[40] How could they guarantee that they could control their desires? Paul was adamant that "a wife must not separate herself from her husband — if she does, she must either remain unmarried or be reunited with her husband — and her husband must not divorce his wife."[41]

The new vogue for celibacy, promoted by Apollos, seems to have been especially appealing to women, as it offered a Heaven-sent opportunity to extract themselves from the prevailing system of serially arranged marriages; no sooner did one husband die than they would be passed on to another. Feminist theologians have castigated Paul for forbidding women to liberate themselves from a life of male dominance and childbearing.[42] It is true that Paul may not have appreciated fully the position of the Corinthian women. But his overriding goal in this letter was to stop people from turning away from the community to enjoy a life of private contemplation. He was not issuing timeless directives to be observed by women living two thousand years later. Because he was convinced that the Parousia was imminent, he would have been horrified by such an idea. Paul was simply addressing the specific and peculiar situation that had arisen in Corinth in the summer of 53. Furthermore in this chapter of this letter, he scrupulously advocated equal rights for men and women in marriage: "The husband must give the wife what is due to her and equally the wife must give the husband his due. The wife cannot claim her body as her own; it is her husband's. Equally the husband cannot claim her body as his own; it is his wife's."[43] Paul was not a fan of the married state. He believed that because "the world as we know it is passing away," it was probably better for both men and women not to burden themselves with the responsibilities of marriage. But he made it clear that this was simply his personal view, not a revealed doctrine, binding on all the faithful for all time.[44]

Two passages in this letter, however, are often quoted to prove that Paul was a die-hard misogynist, the most notorious being his command that women remain silent in public:

> As in all congregations of God's people, women should keep silent at the meeting. They have no permission to talk, but should keep their place as the law directs. If there is something they want to know, they can ask their husbands at home. It is a shocking thing for a woman to talk at the meeting.[45]

This, of course, directly contradicts Paul's insistence that "in Christ" there should be full gender equality. So glaring is this discrepancy that many scholars believe that this passage was inserted into Paul's letter at a later date by those who wanted to make Paul conform more closely to Greco-Roman norms. Paul's letters were copied assiduously after his death and survived in 779 manuscripts dating from the third to the sixteenth century.[46] There are variant versions in the earliest manuscripts of this letter, and copyists appear to have sometimes added remarks that reflected their own opinions rather than the apostle's. One of these is almost certainly the passage quoted above.[47] First, it jars with Paul's care to accord men and women equal rights and duties earlier in this very letter, and it is strange to hear Paul of all people appealing to the authority of "the law." But there are also textual reasons for its later insertion. In the earliest manuscripts, which date only to the third century, it appears in different places, and in its current position it interrupts — almost in midsentence — Paul's argument about spiritual gifts, which continues seamlessly immediately afterward.

The second text quoted to prove Paul's chronic chauvinism is the long, meandering argument for women to cover their heads while praying or prophesying during community meetings.[48] It is interesting that here Paul seems to have no problem about women speaking in public. Again, the passage under discussion interrupts his argument. In the preceding chapter, he had described the way the community should behave at regular meals and, in the interests of unity, urged the Corinthians to avoid offending other people's dietary sensibilities. Then comes this entirely unrelated discussion of women's headgear, which has no connection with what comes before or afterward, and then immediately the discussion of community meals continues, this time focusing on the Lord's Supper. Again, Paul's insistence on male authority in this disputed text is at odds with both his theory and practice of gender equality, and the rhetoric, with its insistence on traditional "practices," is quite alien to Paul and has more in common with the second-century Deutero-Pauline letters to Titus and Timothy.[49]

The American scholar Stephen J. Patterson, however, accepts the authenticity of this passage, pointing out that it does not require women to wear an Islamic-style hijab, but is concerned about male and female hairstyles. He suggests that the Corinthians were taking the baptismal cry — "Neither male nor female" — to an extreme. Men were growing their hair, while women were wearing theirs loose, instead of tying it back in a bun or donning the headdress prescribed for respectable women. Consequently all members of the congregation were sporting long, flowing locks, and it was impossible to distinguish males from females. Paul, Patterson argues, agreed with the Corinthians' theology but argued that blurring the gender distinction was wrong, because it was not what God had ordained at the creation.[50] At this time, the women who were traveling with the peripatetic Stoic philosophers cut their hair short and wore men's clothes to avoid being molested on the road. Paul may have been suggesting that women did not have to look like men when they preached or prayed, as if the male were the human norm, but should do so as themselves.[51]

After this contested passage, the extant text continues with Paul's plea for harmony at the Lord's Supper. Apparently rich patrons, who were paying for the meal and providing the venue, were arriving early and enjoying the choicest portions of food and wine so that there was nothing left for the slaves and artisans who arrived later after discharging their duties.[52] The author of the New Testament letter attributed to James, Jesus's brother, gives us a glimpse of what could happen when a community attracted the attention of a rich patron. He imagines a rich man and a poor man arriving at the Lord's Supper at the same time. The well-dressed man is escorted immediately to a prime seat while the poor man is told to "stand over there, or sit on the floor by my footstool." The author is appalled: Had not God chosen the poor to possess the Kingdom? Yet here the poor were relegated to the margins, while their rich patrons and oppressors were held in honor.[53]

Paul had exactly the same reaction when he heard what was happening in Corinth. "Are you so contemptuous of the community of God that you shame its poorer members?" he demanded. People were bringing their own food; so that some had too much to drink, while others had nothing. Instead of celebrating the unity of the congregation, they fell "into sharply divided groups." He sternly reminded the Corinthians that the Supper was a commemoration of the death of the Lord and looked forward to his return. It evoked the cross and the Messiah's kenosis, so such posturing was entirely out of place. Anyone who behaved in this way "eats and drinks judgment on himself if he does not discern the body."[54] Here Paul was not talking about a denial of transubstantiation or the real presence of Christ in the Eucharist. In this letter, the "body" is always the community; those who do not recognize the sacred core of community, in which the Messiah is present in all members, have failed to acknowledge the Lord himself.

To counter the pretensions of the *pneumatikoi,* Paul cast himself as the direct opposite of this "spiritual aristocracy." Where they presented themselves as "wise," "clever," "strong," and "powerful," he pointed out that he had arrived in Corinth, after suffering humiliation and harassment in Macedonia, "in weakness, in fear, in great trepidation."[55] In all his letters to the Corinthians, Paul emphasized the frailty, humility, and powerlessness of the crucified Messiah. There must be no trying to impress with "clever arguments" or "boasting" of one's spiritual attainments.[56] "Make no mistake about this: if there is anyone among you who fancies himself wise — wise, I mean, by the standards of this age — he must become a fool if he is to be truly wise. For the wisdom of this world is folly in God's sight."[57]

When he responded to the arguments of those who felt free to eat meat sacrificed to idols, therefore, Paul urged them not to glory in the strength of their convictions but to respect the beliefs of the "weaker" members of the community who believed such practices to be wrong. Yes, the *pneumatikoi* were theologically correct: These idols did not exist so there was no logical reason to refrain from this food. But that did not give the "strong" the right to flaunt their advanced and progressive views so aggressively that they upset their brothers and sisters in Christ.[58] If they imitated the kenosis of Jesus, they would not assert their rights in this way. He, Paul, for example, had the right to accept economic support for his mission, but instead he chose to earn his living by manual labor so as not to burden others.[59]

The same principle applied to an ostentatious display of the gifts of the Spirit. The "spirituals" believed that their ability to utter inspired words or speak in tongues proved their superior status, but they were wrong to imagine that they had already attained perfection. Until the Parousia, all these gifts — knowledge (*gnosis*), prophecy, and tongues — were only "partial" versions of what was to come. Our full liberation from frailty and mortality had not yet been attained but was simply a hope for the future. In a later letter, Paul would argue that the ecstatic, incoherent babble of glossolalia was actually a sign of weakness rather than strength: "We do not even know how we ought to pray, but through our inarticulate groans the Spirit himself is pleading for us."[60] And in the last resort, all these gifts were worthless if they were not imbued with love: "I may speak in tongues of men or of angels, but if I have no love I am a sounding gong or a clanging cymbal."[61] The gifts of tongues, miracles, heroic deeds, revelations, spiritual gnosis, and even a heroic martyrdom were of no value if they were not imbued with agape, a self-emptying commitment to the community. This "love" was not simply a warm glow in the heart; it had to be expressed in practical actions that edified — built up — the congregation. That was why Paul believed that prophecy was a greater gift than glossolalia. When somebody spoke in tongues, nobody understood what was being said, but prophecy could speak directly to the heart of others. So "speaking in tongues may build up the speaker himself, but it is prophecy that builds up the Messiah's community."[62]

At the end of his letter, Paul attacked the conviction of the *pneumatikoi* that because they were already immortal, "there is no resurrection of the dead."[63] To imagine that one was already perfect and entirely fulfilled was dangerous. It gave people the illusion that they could do whatever they liked — sleep with prostitutes, engage in incestuous unions, and ignore the poor at the Lord's Supper — because they were inherently faultless, an attitude that led to moral bankruptcy and reduced faith to an ego trip. Worst of all, it entirely subverted the meaning of Jesus's death. So to bring the "spirituals" down to earth, Paul reminded them that their movement was not a nebulous quest for ecstasy and other exotic states of mind. Rather, it was rooted in historical events. Jesus had died a terrible death and had been raised physically to God's right hand. He listed those who had seen the risen Christ — Peter, the Twelve, the five hundred brethren, James, and, lastly, he himself. Jesus's death may have changed the course of history, but the process was not yet complete. It was only when Jesus returned at the Parousia that "we shall all be changed" and "death be swallowed up in victory."[64] Then and only then would Christ establish the Kingdom, "deposing every sovereignty, authority, and power."[65]

Before closing, Paul announced a new project that would occupy him for the rest of his active life. He could see now that his *ekklesiai* were vulnerable. They were easily led astray and needed firm grounding in the first principles of the Jesus movement, which had originally concentrated on building mutually supportive communities as an alternative to the oppressive imperial order. His congregations had to be brought down to earth, and instead of retreating into a private spiritual haze, people had to realize and express their profound connection with one another. They needed to be reminded of the historical roots of their faith to stop them wafting off on airy spiritual adventures. So Paul decided to start a collection for the Jerusalem community. At the Jerusalem conference, he had promised the Pillars to "remember the poor," the *evionim*. Collecting goods to alleviate their hardship would not only show James that his mission had indeed borne fruit, but it would help his communities to order their priorities.

He had already started the collection in Galatia. His disciples there had been reassured by his letter and abandoned their plans to convert to Judaism. Every week after the Sunday meeting, all members of the *ekklesia* would contribute whatever they could afford — a coin, a trinket, a piece of jewelry, or an heirloom — gradually amassing a hoard that in due course would be conveyed to Jerusalem. This weekly reminder of the Holy City, the site of the Messiah's death and resurrection, would help the Galatians develop a new and independent relationship with Israel. Paul never envisaged the collection as a kind of tribute tax paid to a superior congregation; he always referred to it as a "gift" (*charis*) from one messianic congregation to another, each equal in standing.[66]

In his letter, Paul gave the Corinthians the same instructions as he had given the Galatians,[67] in the hope, perhaps, that this practical project would jolt the Corinthians out of their solipsistic introversion and help them cultivate *agape,* a loving, outgoing concern for the poverty of others. The collection would also be a regular reminder that their faith was grounded in a historical event and that they were linked in fellowship to other congregations.[68] It would help to wean the Corinthians from the net of patronage in which they had become enmeshed. Instead of a system in which the poor relied on handouts from the rich, everybody would contribute to the collection as equal participants. It would counter the tributary system of the empire: Instead of wealth being extorted from the provinces and conveyed to the capital, this would be a gift of one group of subject peoples to another.[69] On his next visit, Paul told the Corinthians, he would give letters of introduction to the delegates who would take their offering to Judea. He clearly expected the collection to be ready when he arrived in the city. But circumstances were about to change drastically yet again, and soon the collection would become a new source of contention in Corinth.

The Collection

PAUL'S LETTER to the Corinthians had the desired effect and Timothy was able to report that he had successfully brought the "spirituals" back into the fold and that the congregation was eager to begin the collection. The Corinthians also wanted to maintain a close link with Paul throughout the project and were looking forward eagerly to his next visit. Paul had planned to visit Corinth after his next trip to Macedonia, probably in the autumn of 53, and spend the whole winter there.[1] But he found that he was unable to free himself from his commitments in Asia Minor and sent Titus instead. Even though Titus was warmly received, his Corinthian disciples were deeply hurt, and this disappointment may have contributed to the next crisis in the city.[2]

In the summer of 54, Paul heard that a new group of missionaries of the Jesus movement had established a base in Corinth and was loud in its disapproval of his teaching. Where the "spirituals" had been influenced by the Wisdom movement of Hellenistic Judaism, these new apostles were motivated by the missionary theology developed by some diaspora Jews, which looked forward to a time when the whole world would be converted to Judaism. Israel, they were convinced, would then preside over a new global order of justice and equity; it would be a democracy, but that did not mean government by the perverse and foolish masses, for whom these new missionaries had little time. Instead, the world would be governed by those who best embodied the virtues of the Jewish people. Of great importance to the Jewish missionaries was the "godlike human" (*theios an-thropos*), such as Moses, Elijah, or the Messiah, who embodied true Jewish values and could act as a model and a stimulus to dedicated action.[3]

The new missionaries in Corinth believed that Jesus had been one of these godlike persons and that they themselves also enshrined these superlative Jewish qualities. They argued that Paul's refusal to accept financial support and his decision to work like a common laborer was a tacit admission that his teaching was of little value. He was certainly no *theios anthropos*. On the contrary, they accused him of extorting money from the poor in his collection. Flaunting their own spiritual attainments, the newcomers introduced an aristocratic style of leadership into the Jesus movement that violated all Paul's egalitarian ideals. When he heard this, Paul at once fired off another letter to the Corinthians, vowing to visit them again in the very near future.

Our knowledge of this new development comes from a document known as the Second Epistle to the Corinthians. In fact, this is not a single epistle but a collection of five letters, which are not arranged in chronological order, and with one non-Pauline interpolation. In this correspondence, Paul never mentions the names of his new opponents, but because these slick operators gave themselves such airs, he calls them "super-apostles" and also "sham apostles," confidence tricksters who were all show and no substance and merely masqueraded as emissaries of Christ.[4] They ostentatiously paraded their Jewish credentials, styling themselves "Hebrews," "Israelites," and "Children of Abraham."[5] They exhibited their superior understanding of the Jewish tradition with elaborate and sophisticated allegorical interpretations of scripture, and claimed that their transcendental ecstasies and miracles proved their godlike status. Where Paul had insisted that Jesus's death had marked a break with the past, the super-apostles claimed the seductive glamour of antiquity. They could also produce letters of recommendation to prove that they were the authentic representatives of the Jesus movement, pointing out derisively that Paul had no such credentials.

The super-apostles had fully absorbed the competitive ethos of the Hellenistic world, which celebrated the extraordinary, the astonishing, and the superhuman.[6] The free market economy and the political ideology of the Greco-Roman world were fueled by this fiercely competitive desire for recognition and admiration. This was a miracle culture: inscriptions, poems, and orations all celebrated astounding deeds that filled the populace with amazement. The missionary theology of the super-apostles was also a Jewish version of an imperial theme of universal reconciliation dating back to Alexander the Great, who, according to Plutarch, "thought he had come as both a unifier and a reconciler." Alexander had been determined that "a single law should govern all people, who should look up to a single justice and to a single source of light."[7] Loyal citizens of Rome believed that the Caesars had assumed the mantle of Alexander. In claiming this role for the people of Israel, Jewish missionary theology, like the Jewish Wisdom tradition, was an ideological strategy of a subject people anxious to reclaim a measure of distinction and respect. In Corinth, the super-apostles presented Jesus's astounding miracles and their own exceptional feats as proof of an awe-inspiring power within Judaism that would one day compel the whole world to submit to the "single law" and "single purpose" of Jewish rule.

Paul had countered the claims of Apollos and the "spirituals" by presenting himself as vulnerable and weak. This theme became even more pronounced when he challenged the arrogance of the super-apostles. In the summer of 54, Paul dictated his first attempt to counter their claims.[8] He began by describing himself and his coworkers not as conquering heroes but as prisoners of war carried aloft in Christ's triumphal procession.⁹ They did not need letters of recommendation to the Corinthians, because they were themselves a living testimonial, inscribed indelibly on Paul's heart. He then countered the super-apostles' boastful adulation of their Jewish traditions by reiterating his belief that the written Torah had been replaced by the Spirit, the living presence of God. Again, this was a letter written in response to a set of very particular circumstances; it was not a blanket condemnation of Judaism per se, but, rather, a critique of an interpretation of Judaism that relied on coercive mystique and the exploitation of the extraordinary.

Paul reminded his audience that on Mount Sinai, Moses had stood in the presence of Yahweh, and that when he came down, carrying the tablets of the written law in his hands, his face was illuminated with an unearthly radiance that so stunned the ordinary Israelites "that they would not venture near him." The same thing had happened every time Moses transmitted Yahweh's commandments to the people: "The sons of Israel would see the face of Moses radiant," and when he had finished speaking, he would shield them from this overpowering light by covering himself with a veil.¹⁰ The old law, Paul commented, had been brought to the people with a splendor so dazzling that it filled them with fear and amazement and kept them at a distance. So the revelation (*apocalupsis*) of the Torah had been a "veiling" rather than an "unveiling," and to this day, Paul continued, whenever the law was read aloud, "a veil lies over the mind of the hearer" and its meaning became clear only when interpreted allegorically. But now the Spirit of God had removed that veil and communicated directly with everybody. Instead of the magical trappings of power that had stupefied the people into a dazed acquiescence, there was the liberty of the sons of God.¹¹ Jesus the Messiah did not stand on a lonely eminence that bewildered and alarmed the people; this "divine man" became one with his followers, enabling them to participate in his divine glory: "We all see as in a mirror the glory of the Lord, and we are being transformed into his likeness with ever-increasing glory."[12]

The super-apostles, Paul claimed, had forgotten that Jesus had been crucified. The scandal of his death had made the gospel impossible for those whose minds were blinded by the pomp and magnificence of Caesar, the "god of this passing age." Jesus's true apostles were not supermen but those who exhibited his weakness unto death on the cross. They were hard-pressed, hunted, and struck down: "wherever we go we carry with us in our body the death that Jesus died, so that in this body also the life that Jesus lives may be revealed."[13] It was, therefore, Paul and his companions rather than the super-apostles who were the true representatives of the Christ.[14] Instead of recommending themselves by citing their brilliant accomplishments, they could only display their "steadfast endurance in affliction, hardship, and distress, when they were flogged, imprisoned, mobbed, overworked, sleepless, starving."[15] "Make a place for us in your hearts," Paul begged his converts at the end of the letter. "We have wronged no one, ruined no one, and exploited no one." Whatever happened, the *ekklesia* of Corinth had a permanent place in his heart.[16]

We can imagine the dramatic gestures of the reader who performed Paul's letter in Corinth, as he mimed the veiling and unveiling of the Torah and the people shrinking away in awe and terror. The Corinthians received this performance favorably, but Paul's follow-up visit in person in the autumn of 54 was a disaster. Accustomed now to the oratorical pyrotechnics of the super-apostles, the citizens of Corinth took the general view that Paul cut a poor figure: "His letters . . . are weighty and powerful; but when he is present he is unimpressive; and as a speaker he is beneath contempt."[17] It seems that Paul was attacked and shamed in front of the entire congregation; he had to stand alone before a tribunal to face charges of financial fraud. He was reprimanded for boasting about his Damascus commission and for frightening the congregation. He returned to Ephesus shaken and defeated, convinced that his entire mission was in ruins.

Some would have been tempted to respond aggressively to these accusations, but instead Paul merely amplified his claim that true power resided in powerlessness. Weeping copiously, in a state of great distress and anxiety, he dictated to the scribe a new letter, which he called the "letter of tears."[18] Convinced now that he had nothing to lose, he cast himself as a figure of fun, composing a "Fool's Speech," a form of the rhetorical diatribe that used humor to surprise members of the audience into a new perception and make them think seriously about the consequences and implications of their current position. "Let no one take me for a fool," he began, "but if you must, then let me have the privilege of a fool and let me have a little boast like others." He wasn't the only idiot around, because it seemed as though the Corinthians had allowed themselves to be bullied and humiliated by these charlatans. Clearly they suffered fools gladly: "If someone tyrannizes over you, exploits you, gets you in his clutches, puts on airs, and hits you in the face, you put up with it. And you call me a weakling!"[19] He too could swagger like the super-apostles if he wanted to, since he had exactly the same credentials. After all, he too was a Hebrew, an Israelite, and a descendant of Abraham. So what? These sham apostles claimed to be servants of the Messiah, but Paul could outdo them; still speaking as a fool, instead of bragging about his numerous achievements, he listed a catalogue of catastrophe and failure:

> Five times the Jews have given me the thirty-nine stripes; three times I have been beaten with rods; once I was stoned; three times I have been shipwrecked...I have met with

danger from robbers, dangers from my fellow-countrymen, dangers in the town, dangers at sea...I have toiled and drudged and often gone without sleep; I have been hungry and thirsty and have often gone without food. I have suffered from cold and exposure.[20]

This was what a disciple of Christ should boast about! He finished this parodic account by describing his humiliating escape from Damascus, when he had been bundled ignominiously by his friends into a laundry basket and bumped down the city walls.[21]

Moving from his apostolic qualifications to his spiritual accomplishments, Paul refused to use his rhetorical skills to overwhelm and stupefy his audience into a state of bovine admiration. Instead, he told the story of his marvelous mystical flight through the heavens like a fool, stammering and hesitating oafishly; instead of enthralling his audience about his visions with the smooth confidence of his adversaries, his account was riddled with uncertainty. Was he in the body or out of it? He hadn't a clue. Did he reach the highest heaven? Who knows? But at the end, Paul forced the Corinthians to consider whether it was appropriate to boast about such experiences. While he was in this state, he told them, he "heard words so secret that human lips may not repeat them." The only thing he would boast about was his weakness, and "this would not be the boast of a fool for I should be speaking the truth."[22] To prevent him from being unduly elated by these revelations, like the super-apostles, God had inflicted him with a "thorn in the flesh." Was this a temptation? Or a bodily sickness? Paul would not say; he would repeat only what God had told him: "Power is most fully seen in weakness." Here he rested his case: "for when I am weak, then I am strong."[23]

Shortly after he had dispatched his "letter of tears," Paul's fortunes plummeted to a new low. Claudius's last years had been clouded by court intrigues, and in October 54, he was poisoned by his wife and succeeded by Nero, his adopted seventeen-year-old son. The accession of the new emperor was hailed with relief and joy and an empire-wide resurgence of the imperial cult. But Rome was in trouble: The Parthians threatened the eastern frontier and there were uprisings in Judea. Scapegoats were needed, and Marcus Junius Silanus, governor of Asia, was murdered by Nero's agents on suspicion of treason and, in a roundup of local malcontents, Paul was imprisoned in Ephesus. Luke, always the champion of Rome and reluctant to admit that Paul was ever regarded as an enemy of the empire, tells us nothing of this. Instead, he claims that Paul's mission in Ephesus came to an end after a riot in the Temple of Artemis, when the silversmiths who crafted figurines of the goddess accused him of putting them out of business by undermining the cult.[24]

For a time, the death penalty was a distinct possibility and Paul came close to despair. "The burden of it was far too heavy for us to bear," he wrote later, "so heavy that we even despaired of life."[25] But as the weeks passed, his mood lifted. His beloved Philippians organized a collection and sent Epaphroditas to Ephesus with money to bribe the jailers to ensure that Paul got better rations and treatment. Paul also became aware that because of his imprisonment, the gospel was being widely discussed, even by officials in the imperial guard, and that members of the Jesus movement had felt emboldened "to speak the word of God fearlessly and with extraordinary courage." True, his opponents spoke merely "out of rivalry and competition" and to cause him pain. But who cared? Either way, the gospel was being proclaimed. Writing to acknowledge the Philippians' gift, he told them that he had recovered his equilibrium, and was confident that "I shall never have to admit defeat, but that now as always I shall have the courage for Christ to be glorified in my body, whether the verdict be life or death."[26]

The Philippians' generosity made him see the collection

for Jerusalem in a new light. The super-apostles had shown him that egotism and ambition within the movement could be just as damaging as the injustice of the imperial authorities. He quoted the Christ Hymn to the Philippians, reminding them to avoid this attitude by imitating the Messiah's kenosis in their daily lives. He thanked them for their gift but deliberately diverted attention from the material donation and, rather churlishly perhaps, insisted that in fact he did not need such help: "I have learned to be self-sufficient whatever my circumstances."[27] It was the spirit in which the offering had been made that pleased him. From the very beginning, he told the Philippians, they had understood the ethic of "giving and receiving," which had been central to Jesus's mission in Galilee. Their gift was an expression of agape. But it was also an act of worship, "a fragrant offering [*leitourgia*], an acceptable sacrifice, pleasing to God," and he knew that God would respond with like generosity.[28] This insight would color all Paul's future thinking about the collection.[29]

Paul was released from prison in the spring or summer of 55. We do not know why or how this came about. Perhaps Prisca and Aquila, who, he said later, had risked their lives for him, helped him to escape. Clearly he could not linger in Ephesus, so he set off at once for Troas, where he hoped to preach the gospel.[30] But he was desperate to hear news from Corinth. Had the "letter of tears" sent just before his incarceration won the Corinthians over? Titus had already set off for Corinth to see what had happened, so Paul journeyed to Macedonia to meet him. But there too he found trouble, "fights without and fears within."[31] It seems that the old issue of circumcision had surfaced yet again and that some of his Macedonian followers were seriously considering full conversion to Judaism. He wrote another letter to the Philippians urging them strongly to pay no heed to those who tried to force circumcision on them.[32] But Paul had no time to be depressed by this setback, because Titus arrived with the great news that somehow — either by Titus's intervention or the Corinthians' own initiative — the super-apostles had been vanquished and his converts were anxious to make peace with Paul. "He has told us how you long for me," Paul wrote to the Corinthians in his "letter of reconciliation,"[33] "and how eager to take my side."[34] He realized that his letter had hurt them and knew that they had met Titus in "fear and trembling" and were ready to do anything he asked.[35] In fact, Paul concluded, the experience had made them stronger than ever: "You bore your pain in God's way and just look at the results: it made you take the matter seriously and vindicate yourselves . . . It aroused your devotion and your eagerness to see justice done! At every point you have cleared yourselves of blame."[36]

Not long after this unexpected development, Paul could tell the Corinthians in his next letter that the Macedonians' troubles had also evaporated. They had endured a time of trial, "yet in all this they have been so exuberantly happy that from the depths of their poverty they have shown themselves thoroughly open-handed." They were now eager to contribute to the collection, "going to the limits of their resources, as I can testify, and even beyond that limit and of their own initiative."[37] Paul now urged the Corinthians to resume the project. They had made such a good beginning and were now so rich in "faith, speech, knowledge, and diligence . . . as well as in the love you have for us" that they should be equally lavish in this generous service (*leitourgia*) of God.[38] The joy that Paul repeatedly expressed at this time was not simply a feeling of happiness but delight in the company and activities of members of the Jesus movement, a sign of the Spirit that heralded the advent of a new world.[39] The project of the collection had stalled disastrously for a time, but it had now gained an irresistible momentum.[40]

Titus went to Corinth to organize the collection with two companions whose names we do not know, even though one of them was highly respected in the movement. Because such "large sums" were involved, Paul insisted that the collection be managed by people of unblemished reputation.⁴¹ Paul was now thinking ahead to its reception in Jerusalem. How could this act of gratuitous generosity fail to persuade James and the more conservative Judeans that his gentile converts were indeed inspired by the Spirit of God? In yet another letter, included in the Corinthian corpus but in fact addressed to all the *ekklesiai* in Achaea,⁴² Paul described the collection as a manifestation of the body of Christ, which demonstrated the way all its members supported one another and united the entire Jesus movement. After years of bitter strife, this unity was a gift of God, and their gift to the *evionim* would return to God as a sacrifice equal to any of the offerings made in the temple.

Paul was now convinced that the collection would hasten the coming of the Kingdom, so he decided that it should be delivered as soon as possible. Isaiah had foreseen the procession of gentiles to the Holy City in the Last Days, bearing rich gifts from every region of the world. It seemed almost as if the prophet were speaking directly to James and his congregation of *evionim:*

> *Lift up your eyes and look around;*
> *All are assembling and coming towards you . . .*
> *At this sight you will grow radiant*
> *Your heart throbbing and full*
> *Since the riches of the sea will flow to you*
> *The wealth of the nations come to you.*⁴³

But the collection was not an acknowledgment of Jerusalem's leadership of the movement; nor was it an act of patronage in which a more prosperous community gave a helping hand to "the poor" as an assertion of its superiority. These kinds of distinctions had no place in the Messiah's community. "It is a question of equality [*isotes*]," Paul insisted emphatically to the Corinthians. "At the moment, your surplus meets their need, but one day your need may be met from their surplus. The aim is equality."[44] Paul had not used the word *isotes* in his letters before, but this egalitarian spirit had pervaded his entire mission. The Christ's people held all things in common, demonstrating an alternative economy based on sharing and reciprocity in a community of equals.

Paul spent the winter of 55–56 in Greece. He was now convinced that his work in the eastern provinces was complete. This was an extraordinary assumption. How could he possibly imagine that, in a few short years, he had laid the foundation of a global religion? Paul was not stupid; we shall see that he had serious misgivings about the delegation to Jerusalem based on a shrewd appreciation of the difficulties involved. But, of course, he was not thinking in purely pragmatic terms. He was certain that God was at work in the sudden restoration of harmony and in the collection itself. This belief may, perhaps, have been his undoing. Convinced that the gospel must reach "the ends of the earth," as Isaiah had foretold, he now looked westward to Spain, where the Pillars of Hercules stood on the cusp of the world-encircling ocean. In this new phase of his mission, he intended Rome to be the bridgehead of his activities in Europe, so that winter he wrote his epistle to the community of Jesus's followers in the imperial capital.

Paul's letter to the Romans is regarded as his masterpiece and the definitive summation of his theology. But, like his other letters, it is less about doctrine than a social imperative. In one respect, it is different from the rest of his correspondence, because he was writing to a congregation he had never met.[45] We do not know who took the Jesus movement to Rome; there is no historical evidence for the traditional belief that the congregation there was established by Peter. Ever since Luther, this letter has been read as a definitive statement of Paul's groundbreaking doctrine of justification by faith. But recent scholar-

ship has shown that Luther's interpretation does not corre-
spond to Paul's thinking at all, and that far from being central
to Paul's thought, this topic is mentioned only in Paul's letters
to the Galatians and Romans for "the specific and limited purpose of defending the right of gentile converts to be full heirs of
the promises to Israel."[46] There has also been a scholarly retreat
from the widespread assumption that Paul's opponents were always either Jews or "Judaizing" Jewish-Christians.[47] We have
seen that Paul had wider concerns, including a politico-religious
condemnation of the "rulers of this age," a theme that had special poignancy in a letter to the Messiah's followers in the imperial capital.

As usual, Paul began his letter by introducing himself and
greeting its recipients, but this time he was writing in what the
ancients called the "polished style." His tone was grandiloquent
and ambassadorial as he presented himself as the envoy of Jesus,
a royal descendant of the House of David, with a universal mission. His Roman audience would immediately have noted his
appropriation of terms that were prominent in official imperial
theology — terms that are now also familiar to us:

> This gospel God announced beforehand in sacred scriptures
> through his prophets. It is about his Son: on the human level
> he was a descendant of David, but on the level of the spirit —
> the Holy Spirit — he was proclaimed Son of God by an act
> of power that raised him from the dead; it is about Jesus the
> Messiah, our Lord. Through him I received the privilege of
> an apostolic commission to bring people of all nations to
> faith [*pistis*] and obedience in his name.[48]

In the official imperial theology, the titles "Son of God" and
"Lord" usually applied to the emperor and the word "gospel" re-
ferred to his achievements. By speaking of Jesus in these terms,
Paul was tacitly inviting the Roman community to declare its

loyalty to the true ruler of the universe. Members were to become co-conspirators with him in acknowledging that, unbeknownst to the powers that be, a fundamental change had occurred when God had vindicated the crucified Messiah.[49]

When Paul spoke of the apostolic commission bringing "people of all nations to *pistis*," he did not mean, of course, "belief" but "loyalty." In official imperial theology, Caesar represented the *pistis* of Rome — Rome's fidelity to treaty obligations and the rule of law, Rome's conviction of righteousness, confidence, veracity, and rectitude. The term appeared frequently on coins and inscriptions.[50] Yet when the word was applied to ordinary folk, *pistis* simply meant the loyalty that subjects owed to the emperor. As in his previous letters, Paul reversed these expectations. His "gospel" announced "the saving power of God for everyone who has faith — the Jew first, but the Greek also — because in it, the justice [*dikaiosune*] of God is seen at work, beginning in faith and ending in faith."[51]

Paul then embarked on a scathing condemnation of the "impiety and wickedness" of those men and women who refused to recognize the ubiquitous presence of God in the world and behaved as though nothing was sacred.[52] He castigated their idolatry, shameful sexual practices, "wickedness, villainy, greed, and malice." They were guilty of envy, treachery, ambition, arrogance, and insolence because of the chronic egotism that made them see themselves as the center of the universe rather than God. This assault is often interpreted as a standard Jewish denunciation of the evils of the gentile world, and, indeed, Paul tacitly acknowledged that this kind of rhetoric was indeed common in the synagogue. But Jews were not alone in decrying the evils of the time. Roman writers and politicians of all persuasions agreed that Roman civilization was in decline and that theirs was a "godless age."[53] "What does corrupting time not diminish?" Horace lamented. "Our grandparents have weaker heirs; we have degenerated further and soon will beget offspring more wicked yet."[54] It was this fear that caused an empire-wide eruption of hope every time a new emperor was acclaimed, as if this time, finally, this endemic immorality might be reversed.[55]

Paul was denouncing the evils of the day in this larger context. He may have had the Jewish super-apostles in mind when he spoke of "rivalry, treachery, and malevolence; gossips and scandalmongers" who were "insolent, arrogant, and boastful."[56] He may also have been thinking of the imperial household when he lambasted current sexual perversions, since there was much rumor about the vice of the court and the wicked scheming of its women. Had not Claudius been murdered by his wife? Not even the Caesars, hailed as "divine humans," guardians of Roman *pistis* and upholders of Roman law, were exempt from this widespread corruption. Jews and gentiles alike proclaimed their belief in a law that ordered society and represented the will of God, yet everybody without exception was guilty of transgression. This grim diatribe introduced Paul's reflection on the role of law and, as in his letter to the Galatians, he was considering law in general, not merely the Torah. Despite its promises, law could not save humanity from toxic social injustice; class, ethnic, and social divisions; and moral and political chaos.[57]

In a rhetorical trope, Paul then focused on an imaginary Jewish member of his audience in the Roman congregation, who had listened to this catalogue of sins and, assuming that this was just another of the usual Jewish condemnations of the gentile world, felt a smug glow of righteousness. But Paul nipped that in the bud: "You have no defense, then, whoever you may be, when you sit in judgment," he told him, "for in judging others you condemn yourself, since you, the judge, are equally guilty."[58] Could anyone — Jew or gentile — claim to be truly free of any or all of the crimes that Paul had just listed in the privacy of his or her heart? "None will be justified before God by hearing the law but only by doing it."[59] God had no favorites. Paul insisted that anybody, Jew or gentile, who claimed to be superior to others had lost the plot because God was the God equally of everybody, of Jews and Greeks alike.[60] In this rhetorical appeal to a Jew in his audience, Paul was using Jewish chauvinism as an example of all reliance on privilege and status.[61] "All alike have sinned . . . What room then is left for human pride?"[62] Jews who passed judgment on pagans, Jewish followers of Jesus who belittled and denigrated gentile members of the *ekklesia,* Roman citizens who regarded Jews as an inferior subject race, or members of the aristocratic elite who believed that their inherited position entitled them to lord it over the hoi polloi — all would come under God's judgment when he intervened to bring this age to an end.

As Paul had claimed in his letter to the Galatians, law divided people into classes, nations, and genders, privileging some and suppressing others, so that Jews felt loftier than Greeks and vice versa; Romans felt inherently superior to barbarians, freedmen to slaves, and men to women. What Paul called "law" mirrored not only God's will but the collective will of society, which made demands on individuals that caused them to feel acutely aware of their failings and weaknesses, made them compulsively seek personal honor and recoil in horror from public shame.[63] "Law brings only consciousness of sin," Paul explained.[64] When Paul spoke of his own sin, he always remembered his persecution of Jesus's followers. At his conversion, he had suddenly realized: "I do not do the good that I want." His zealous obedience to the law had not hastened the coming of the Messiah but had actually impeded it. The cause of this was not the law itself but "the sin that has its dwelling in me."[65] Paul was not complaining about his inability to fulfill the law, as Luther imagined. For Paul, the "sin" that had made him persecute the Messiah's community was egotism, a desire to assert his own desires and boost his own status at the expense of others. He had transformed the law into a means of gaining honor for himself and his group.[66] To seek privilege and distinction in this way was to deny the law's very essence by aspiring to godlike status.

Paul had seen the danger of this kind of chauvinism again and again during his mission. It had surfaced disastrously in Antioch, when the "messengers from James" had made his Jewish colleagues withdraw from table fellowship with their gentile brothers and sisters out of a mistaken sense of superiority. Something similar had made his Galatian converts feel inferior to "proper" Jews. In Corinth, both the "spirituals" and the super-apostles had been in quest of a spurious sense of prestige. Paul knew how seductive this could be from his own experience; that was why he had insisted that the best way to eradicate "sin" was in the daily kenosis required in myriad practical ways in a mutually supportive community in which all were equals.

In his correspondence with the Corinthians, Paul had called this "sinful" attitude "boasting" (*kanchusthai*). When addressing the hypothetical Jew who believed that the Torah gave him an unshakable advantage over gentiles, Paul told him:

> You take pride in your God; taught by the law, you know what really matters; you are confident that you are a guide to the blind, a light to those in darkness, an instructor of the foolish, and a teacher of the immature, because you possess in the law the embodiment of knowledge and truth.[67]

But Roman gentiles felt equally righteous when confronted with a man convicted, disgraced, and executed by Roman law for the slightest misdemeanor. The spirit of "boasting" led to "the works of the law," which were social differentiation, aggressive competition, greed, conflict, and disunity.[68]

Sin had come into the world with Adam's egotistic self-assertion and his refusal to accept limits: At the serpent's suggestion, he had aspired to be "like a god" and brought misery into the world.[69] Writing to the Philippians, Paul had suggested that a new humanity had come into being with the Messiah, who, unlike the Caesars, "did not think equality with God a thing to be grasped at" but had "emptied himself" of such ambition, chauvinism, and self-preoccupation and become nothing. Relinquishing the protection of privilege, he had accepted "even death on a cross." Paul had shown the Galatians a Messiah who had voluntarily put himself under the curse of the law in solidarity with all those ostracized by legal systems that degraded some and elevated others. To the Corinthians, Paul had preached the collective, participatory nature of this salvation, since all the faithful formed the body of Christ. Now to the Roman congregation, Paul presented Jesus as a king who, astonishingly, had joined the rebels who broke the law:

> We were still helpless when at his appointed moment Christ died for sinful men. It is not easy to die, even for a good man — though of course for someone really worthy, a man might be prepared to die — but what proves that God loves us is that Christ died for us while we were still sinners.[70]

Christ, to whom the imperial title "son of God" truly belonged, had turned the prevailing norms of the political world on their head. He was the direct counterpart of the Caesar, who called himself *primus inter pares* ("first among equals"). Jesus's vindication by God had brought to an end the one-sided notion of *pistis*, which had meant the enforced loyalty of subjects to their masters. The Kyrios Jesus had embraced weakness rather than privilege and a solidarity based on equality rather than alienation and coercion. Hence the Messiah's followers had been liberated from domination by the Spirit, which was "not the spirit of slavery, leading you back into a life of fear," but that which brought them into the "glorious liberty of the sons of God."[71] Yet Paul was careful to warn the Romans against the errors of the Corinthian "spirituals" who had believed that they were already perfected human beings. Until the Parousia, human beings remained subject to suffering and mortality, though they could be confident of their final victory.[72]

But as Paul's letter drew to a close, he added some instructions, which, on first reading, seemed to contradict all that had gone before. The intrepid opponent of empire now insisted:

> Every person must submit to the authorities in power, for all authority comes from God, and the existing authorities are instituted by him. It follows that anyone who rebels against authority is resisting a divine institution . . . You wish to have no fear of the authorities? Then continue to do right and you will have their approval, for they are God's agents working for your good . . . That is why you are obliged to submit.[73]

This passage seems to contradict Paul's overall message so blatantly that some scholars believe it to be a later addition.[74] Others accept its authenticity but argue that it must be read against the backdrop of Paul's conviction of Christ's imminent return to judge this imperial world. Until that time, Roman rule was God's will but God's support of the status quo was only temporary and would be abrogated when Christ dragged the mighty from their thrones.[75]

Paul had never been a rabble-rouser. He had told the Thessalonians to live quietly and attend to their business. Nothing must be done that might lead the authorities to a massive repression of the Messiah's followers, since this would impede the coming of the Kingdom. Memories of Claudius's expulsion of some members of the Jesus movement were still fresh in Rome. Paul was relying on the Roman *ekklesia* to support his mission in the West and did not want any risk to its survival.[76] Others point out that in this passage Paul was quoting from a fragment of Jewish tradition that dated back to the days of the Roman republic, before the establishment of the empire. By deliberately quoting this now obsolete piece of legislation, Paul gave it a critical slant, tacitly urging decentralization and undermining the ideology that identified the state as inseparable from the Caesar.[77]

It is, however, surely significant that Paul immediately insisted that political as well as ethical activity must be submitted to the overriding commandment of agape: "Love your neighbor as yourself." "Love cannot avenge a neighbor; therefore, love is the fulfillment of the law."[78] In his interpretation of this commandment, Jesus had taught his disciples that they had to love even their enemies and persecutors, just as God allowed the sun to shine and the rain to fall on good and wicked people alike.[79] As always in Paul's teaching, "unity" and "solidarity" were the watchwords. Political hatred, with its concomitant sense of righteous superiority, had no place in the Messiah's community.

Paul then went on to insist to the Romans, as he had to the Corinthians, that the "strong" must not damage the conscience of the "weak." He had already warned Jewish members of the congregations against an ingrained tendency to look down on pagans, but it seems that in the Roman community gentile members had developed a chauvinism toward Jews, who, they claimed, had rejected the Messiah and irretrievably lost God's favor.[80] This may have inspired Paul's passionate defense of the Jewish people in chapters nine to eleven of this letter, where he identified strongly with his own people. Their plight, he insisted, "was a great grief and unceasing sorrow" in his heart:

> I would even pray to be an outcast myself, cut off from Christ, if it would help my brothers, my kinsfolk by natural descent. They are descendants of Israel, chosen to be God's sons; theirs is the glory of the divine presence, theirs the covenants, the law, the temple worship, and the promises. The patriarchs are theirs, and from them by natural descent came the Messiah.[81]

Paul could not believe that God had rejected his people forever. But he pointed out that it was only because of their "false step" in rejecting the Messiah that salvation had come to the gentiles. He was convinced that God had a secret plan: The apparent hardening of Israel's heart would last only "until the gentiles have been admitted in full strength; once that has happened the whole of Israel will be saved."[82]

But in the meantime, the gentile members of the *ekklesia* must not look down on those Jewish members who still observed the Torah's dietary regulations. Roman citizens in the community may have retained their view of Jews as an inherently subject race and regarded their ancient customs as barbaric. Paul, as we know, no longer believed such practices to be essential, but the law of love ruled out any such chauvinism, since all in the Messiah's family were God's servants. "Let us therefore cease judging one another but rather make up our own minds to place no obstacle or stumbling block in a fellowbeliever's way... If a fellow-believer is outraged by what you eat then you are no longer guided by love."[83]

Paul had devoted years of his life to bringing the gentiles to God, as the scriptures had foretold. He now shared with the Romans his plans for the Western mission and told them that he hoped to visit them on his way to Spain. This gave him the opportunity to introduce the topic of the collection, which underlined the unity of Jew and gentile in the Messiah's community:

> Macedonia and Achaea have resolved to raise a fund for the benefit of the poor among God's people at Jerusalem. They have resolved to do so, and indeed are under an obligation to them. For if the Jewish believers shared their spiritual treasures with the Gentiles, the Gentiles have a clear duty to contribute to their material needs.[84]

Years earlier, Paul had promised the Pillars that he would "re-member the poor" in Jerusalem and support them in their es-chatological task of preparing for Jesus's return to the Holy City. But after his long mission among the gentiles, he no longer accepted the Jerusalem congregation's estimation of itself as an exceptional community. He now described the collection to the Romans as an initiative of his gentile communities and a recip-rocal exchange of gifts.

Paul may have entrusted his letter to Phoebe, leader of the *ekklesia* in Cenchreae, Corinth's eastern seaport, who had busi-ness in Rome.[85] He then devoted himself to organizing the grand delegation to Jerusalem to ensure that it was ready to leave in the spring of 56. The goal was to arrive in the Holy City in time for the celebration of the festival of Weeks in the tem-ple. Paul had mixed feelings. On the one hand, he was confi-dent that the expedition would be a success. Despite the tension between himself and James since the Antioch dispute, he could not imagine that the Jerusalem community would fail to recog-nize the simple goodness of his gentile converts. His assemblies had struggled through many difficulties and Paul believed that they had now acquired a weight of their own. It would be a large delegation — Luke suggests that the numbers were too great for all the delegates to travel and lodge together.[86] It would cer-tainly demonstrate the power the Jesus movement had acquired in the diaspora as a result of Paul's mission. His converts were no longer enmeshed in a self-indulgent quest for personal ful-fillment but were becoming ever more aware that they formed a global community. The collection would demonstrate their commitment to working side by side, as equals, with "the poor" of Jerusalem for the coming of the Kingdom.[87]

But Paul also had worries, which he had shared with the Ro-man congregation: "Pray to God for me that I might be saved from unbelievers in Judea and that my errand in Jerusalem may find acceptance with God's people."[88] He knew that the extraordinary spectacle of a large procession of foreigners bearing gifts to the City of Zion would certainly remind Jewish worshippers of Isaiah's vision of an End Time pilgrimage to the Holy City, "when the riches of the sea will flow to you, the wealth of the nations come to you."[89] In his letter to the Romans, Paul quoted Isaiah's celebration of the future conversion of gentiles to the God of Israel: "How beautiful on the mountains are the feet of one who brings good news, who heralds peace, brings happiness, proclaims salvation, and tells Zion: 'Your God is King!'"[90] Yet he also knew that this oracle had begun with Yahweh's promise to Jerusalem: "Clothe yourself in strength, Zion ... since no longer shall there enter you either the uncircumcised or the unclean."[91] But he would be bringing a crowd of uncircumcised and non-Torah-observant gentiles into this sacred city on one of the holiest days in the Jewish year.

Paul knew perfectly well that he was turning the predicted eschatological scenario on its head.[92] When he had promised the Pillars at the end of the Jerusalem Conference that he would "remember the poor," he had won acceptance for his gentile mission as equal to Peter's mission to the Jews, but by now he was convinced that it was *more* important than the Jewish mission. In his letter to the Romans, Paul had told the gentile members of the community that he was proud to have been commissioned to bring the gospel to the gentiles. "But let me tell you pagans this," he had insisted. "The purpose of it is to make my own people envious of you, and in this way save some of them."[93] The "messengers" whom he was bringing to Jerusalem would not be leading the scattered Jewish communities back to Zion, as the prophets had foretold. Nor were these gentiles going to live in Zion under Jewish law; they were going to disperse again and take the gospel all over the world. Jerusalem was no longer the epicenter of the movement, and his gentiles were not meekly bearing gifts to the temple, as Isaiah had predicted, but were taking the collection to a vulnerable Jewish sect that called itself "the poor." Paul knew only too well that his delegation would be exactly the kind of irritant that might excite the "envy" and resentment of his fellow Jews, but, against all odds, he hoped that it would force them to see the error of their ways.

In his account, Luke does not even mention the collection and, as usual, Acts must be approached with caution. But there is no reason to doubt the general outline of the journey as described by Luke. He tells us that Paul and some of the delegates spent Passover in Philippi and then sailed down the coast of Asia, traversed Phoenicia, and finally arrived at the port of Caesarea, making the last leg of the trip by land. But it is unlikely that Paul's meeting with James was as cordial as Luke suggests. He described James and the elders giving the new arrivals "a very warm welcome"; after asking Paul "for a detailed account of all that God had done among the pagans through his ministry, they gave glory to God when they heard this."[94] Paul was notorious in the movement, and James and his community would have had no need to be informed about his activities. And far from being moved to praise God for his presence, they probably felt that he had put them in an impossible position.[95]

After the persecution of Herod Agrippa, James had won the respect of the most devout inhabitants of the Holy City by his piety and assiduous Torah observance. He had thus secured the position of the Jesus movement in Jerusalem. But the arrival of this large group of gentiles who claimed to have inherited the promises to Abraham would certainly be regarded as inflammatory by the mainstream Jewish population, and the *evionim* would probably bear the brunt of this displeasure. To make matters worse, Paul had unwittingly arrived at a particularly dangerous moment. Seven weeks earlier, an unnamed prophet, known as "the Egyptian," had marched a crowd of thirty thousand dissidents through the desert to the Mount of Olives, "ready to force an entry into Jerusalem, overwhelm the Roman garrison, and seize supreme power."[96] Needless to say, the Romans had ruthlessly put this uprising down, but the Egyptian had escaped and was still at large. So the Romans were ready for trouble, especially during the harvest festival of Weeks, which celebrated Yahweh's kingship of the Land of Israel, a cultic reminder that both the land and its produce belonged to Yahweh and not to Rome.

Paul's grand enterprise seems to have been such a dismal failure that Luke either knew nothing about it or wanted to hush it up. Paul's views were well known in Jerusalem; some of the Pharisee zealots who had backed his persecution of the Jesus movement would still regard him as an apostate and a traitor, and his large entourage of gentiles would have confirmed their darkest suspicions. It would have been compromising and risky for James to accept the gift of the collection unconditionally, but it was equally impossible to turn it down. Not only would this have been extremely insulting to Paul, but also it would certainly have split the Jesus movement irrevocably. Luke's account may represent a compromise solution. He tells us that James persuaded Paul to pay for the elaborate, weeklong purification rites that four devout Jewish members of the *ekklesia* were to perform in the temple and to purify himself in the temple with them on the third and seventh days. This would show everybody that he was not an enemy of the Torah.[97] In this way, James could accept the collection, as it were under the counter, with embarrassment and subterfuge.

But, Luke says, when Paul went into the temple to perform the rites, there was a riot and he was almost lynched. Thinking that he was the missing Egyptian, the Romans took him into custody.[98] Paul was then imprisoned in Caesarea and, according to Luke, his case become the subject of an acrimonious dispute between Felix, the Roman procurator, and Ananias, the high priest, who were locked in a bitter power struggle with each other. Eventually Paul, as a Roman citizen, was extradited to the capital to be tried by the imperial tribunal.

Luke has Paul make many fine speeches in captivity — to the Jewish worshippers in the temple, to Felix and his successor Festus, to the Sanhedrin, and to Herod Agrippa II — inspiring universal acclamation and respect. He describes Paul's journey to Rome as a thrilling adventure, and when he finally arrived, Luke says, the entire community of the Messiah came out to greet him on the Appian Way. Luke concluded his history by saying that for two full years, Paul lived in Rome, proclaiming the Kingdom of God quite openly and without hindrance.[99] Always anxious to show that Paul was the obedient servant of the empire, Luke could not bear to relate the truth — and may not even have known what happened to his hero.

In fact, it seems clear that Paul was effectively silenced. There is no evidence of his founding any more communities after his fatal visit to Jerusalem. If he wrote any more letters, they have not survived. Nobody seems to know how or when Paul died. Writing in about 96 CE, Clement, bishop of Rome, never mentioned his imprisonment in the imperial capital but claimed that he completed his mission to Spain: "He preached in the East and the West, winning a noble reputation for his faith. He taught righteousness to all the world; and after reaching the farthest limits of the West, bearing his testimony before kings and rulers, he passed out of this world and was received into the holy places."[100] The fourth-century church historian Eusebius, bishop of Caesarea, however, believed that Paul was beheaded and Peter crucified in Rome during the persecution of Nero in 64. In support of this tradition, he claimed: "The record is confirmed by the fact that the cemeteries there are still called by the names of Peter and Paul." To make "the truth of my account still more certain," Eusebius also quoted two late second-century authorities: a churchman named Gaius who lived in Rome and Bishop Dionysius of Corinth.[101] But Eusebius seemed to protest too much, uneasily aware that his evidence was flimsy and circumstantial. The facts are probably simpler, and more terrible.

John Dominic Crossan has suggested that the disciples may never have known what really happened to Jesus after his arrest and their flight to safety in Galilee. It is most unlikely that a special nighttime meeting of the Sanhedrin would have been convened during a major festival to decide the fate of an obscure prophet from Nazareth, as the gospels claimed. Nor is it likely that Pilate, who was eventually recalled to Rome because of his reckless cruelty, would have made such valiant efforts to save him. The gospel crucifixion narratives consist of a medley of quotations from the more sorrowful psalms, suggesting that the disciples scoured the scriptures (which they believed had predicted the fate of the Messiah) for clues. "What we have now in those detailed passion accounts is not *history remembered* but *prophecy historicized*," Crossan argues.[102] Jesus was certainly crucified; this is attested by both Josephus and Tacitus. But crucifixions were regular, unremarkable events in the Roman Empire. "I doubt very much if Jewish police and Roman soldiery needed to go too far up the chain of command in handling a Galilean peasant like Jesus," Crossan concludes. "It is hard for us, I repeat, to bring our imagination down low enough to see the casual brutality with which he was probably taken and executed."[103]

Once in Roman custody, Paul could also simply have disappeared. In our own time, we have seen how easily a powerful regime can dispose of small-fry subversives who stand in its way. The fact that there are such variant views of his death indicate that once he was taken into Roman custody, he simply vanished, dispatched like Jesus with "casual brutality." There are a number of ways in which he could have died an obscure, miserable, and degrading death in a Roman prison. If so, we can only wonder whether at the end he finally succumbed to despair. He had not reached the ends of the earth and he had not witnessed the Parousia; his collection had failed and the movement seemed likely to split. And what would Paul have felt had he seen how the church that he helped to create would interpret his teaching?

Afterlife

T HE GENTILE CHURCHES would have been distressed beyond measure by the loss of Paul. So much had been expected of the grand enterprise of the collection, yet it had resulted in a tragic fiasco. They would also have felt lost and cast adrift. Paul had not only been their main link with Jerusalem but had also connected them with one another. Now there was a danger that the unity of the *ekklesiai,* which had been so important to Paul, would disintegrate. The *ekklesiai* would have felt shamed and humiliated by the reception of their gift by the Jerusalem congregation. Their connection with Jerusalem would become even more tenuous after the outbreak of the Jewish War against Rome and the destruction of the temple that had been so central to the piety of James and his community. Judaism would itself be transformed by this catastrophe: The rabbis would convert the temple religion into a religion of the book, creating new scriptures — the Mishnah and the Jerusalem and Babylonian Talmuds — that would take the temple's place and become the locus of the divine. In the process of this great transformation, the Jesus movement in Judaism would slowly dwindle when Jesus failed to return, and what we now call Christianity would become a predominantly gentile faith.

Since the late nineteenth century, a number of scholars have argued that the letters to the Colossians and the Ephesians were written in Paul's name after his death. They have noted that their style differs markedly from Paul's own direct and incisive mode of writing and that they reflect a later period. There is no more anguished discussion about the admission of gentiles into the assembly, and instead of the focus on an individual *ekklesia*, as in Paul's authentic letters, we find an emphasis on the movement as a whole. What we can now call a "church" has emerged, with a theology of its own. Instead of dealing with the particular problems encountered by a specific community, these letters deal with more general matters. They may have been written toward the end of the first century by followers of Paul, who wrote in his name because they believed that during this difficult period, the authority of an apostolic voice was essential.

Because of Paul's disappearance, it was becoming increasingly clear that the Parousia was not going to come as quickly as everybody had thought. Where Paul had urged his disciples to hold aloof from the pagan world because "the world as we know it is passing away," it was now becoming apparent that Jesus's followers faced the prospect of a long-term period of coexistence with mainstream society. How could they achieve this without losing their distinctive identity? Paul had used the collection as a way of bringing his scattered communities together; now his successors had to capitalize on this, taking Paul's teaching into a new phase to meet the demands of a changed world. Hence these two letters take Paul's theology into a new direction.

Both authors have a highly developed consciousness of the church as a whole. In fact, they have invented ecclesiology. They both use Paul's image of the body of Christ—but with one important difference. Paul had subverted imperial theology, which had seen Caesar as the head of the body politick. Instead, he had developed a more pluralistic ideal of an interdependent community, in which the "inferior" parts of the body received greater honor than the head. The authors of Colossians and Ephesians, however, placed Christ at the head of the body, while still trying to preserve some of Paul's original insights. "[Christ] is the head of the body, the church; he is its origin, the first to return from the dead, to become in all things supreme," says the author of Colossians.[1] The author of Ephesians urges his readers, as Paul would have done, to grow up fully into Christ: "He is the head, and on him the whole body depends. Bonded and held together by every constituent joint, the whole frame grows through the proper functioning of each part, and builds itself up through love."[2] There is an attempt to preserve Paul's emphasis on love, on the importance of community building, and on the interdependence of members, but a graded hierarchy was beginning to emerge, with Christ no longer identified with the body as a whole and with everybody in the *ekklesia* but firmly with the head.

In this vision, however, Christ still supplanted Caesar, but after the horror of the Jewish War with Rome, Paul's preoccupation with "the rulers of this age" had been muted. Christ was now presented as vanquishing cosmic rather than earthly powers. Instead of focusing on the imminent Parousia, when Christ would return to earth to subdue the imperial authorities, the authors insisted that Jesus had already achieved that victory but on a celestial plane. When tackling the problems raised by the Corinthian "spirituals," Paul had been adamant that the Kingdom had not yet come. But these authors insisted that Christ's followers were already living the redeemed life. "He has rescued us from the domain of darkness and brought us into the kingdom of his dear Son," writes the author of Colossians; they were already "in the realm of light."[3] "In Christ indeed we have been given our share in the heritage, as was decreed in the design whose purpose is everywhere at work," says the author of Ephesians. Christ was now enthroned "far above all government and authority, all power and domination, and any title of sovereignty that commands allegiance, not only in this age but in the age to come."[4] Paul's strongly political vision had been transposed to another world and another dimension of time.

These letters show the beginning of a Pauline tradition, which was altering Paul's theology and thus enabling it to speak to different circumstances. This is particularly evident in the authors' directions about the Christian household. Paul's utopian egalitarianism had been replaced by a more hierarchical vision, in which wives must obey their husbands, children their fathers, and slaves must "give entire obedience to your earthly masters."[5] Both authors expressed these new ideals in a style and vocabulary that seem stylized; already a tradition of patriarchy that was alien to Paul seems to have been established in the gentile *ekklesiai.* The baptismal cry—"Neither male nor female"—has been subsumed into the hierarchical body of Christ:

> Wives, be subject to your husbands as though to the Lord; for the man is the head of the woman, just as Christ is the head of the church. Christ is, indeed, the savior of that body; but just as the church is subject to Christ, so must women be subject to their husbands in everything.[6]

These conventional instructions reflect the newly felt need to coexist with Greco-Roman society. Now that the Parousia had been indefinitely delayed, Paul the radical had to be reined in if the movement was to survive. These directions conformed closely to the household codes to which Greco-Roman philosophers, historians, and Hellenistic Jewish writers attached great importance, seeing the well-ordered family as crucial to the proper ordering of society.[7] The patriarchal household described here is not, therefore, an invention of either Paul or the Deutero-Paulines but an expression of Greco-Roman norms, which the authors have tried to imbue with the Pauline ideals of love and service; throughout the focal point of loyalty is not the state, as it is in the Hellenistic household codes, but loyalty to Christ.[8]

Paul's radicalism was utopian. It was possible only while everybody believed that Christ would return in the very near future to inaugurate a new world order. Paul's vision of law as unjust and divisive expresses our perennial discontent with civilization and our stubborn conviction, which may date back to the millennia during which we lived as hunter-gatherers in small egalitarian communities, that people are meant to live together as equals. After a mere five thousand years, we may not yet have adapted fully to civilization, which has always been inegalitarian and cannot survive without draconian laws. Yet paradoxically, Paul's vision of Christ dethroning earthly authority had depicted him returning like a conquering emperor:

> Then comes the end, when he delivers up the kingdom to God the Father, after deposing every sovereignty, authority, and power. For he is destined to reign until God has put all enemies under his feet and the last enemy to be deposed is death. Scripture says: "He has put all things in subjection under his feet."[9]

The authors of Colossians and Ephesians preserved this imagery, transposed to the cosmic plane. When the unthinkable happened and Constantine became the first Christian Roman emperor in 312, this rhetoric was at hand to justify his world rule.

The authors of Colossians and Ephesians were anxious to preserve Paul's voice and authority. But to most Christians in the early church, he was a baffling figure. When the author of the Second Epistle of Peter described the Lord's final coming to the communities of the diaspora, he urged them to be patient, as Paul, "our dear friend and brother," had advised in a letter: "He does the same in all his other letters, whenever he speaks about this, though they contain some obscure passages, which the ignorant and unstable misinterpret to their own ruin, as they do the other scriptures."[10] The German scholar Ernst Käsemann once remarked that in the years immediately after his death, Paul was "for the most part unintelligible."[11] He had made very little impression on the second-century theologians known as the Apostolic Fathers. Ignatius of Antioch refers to him only six times and it is clear that his understanding is at best superficial; Polycarp, bishop of Smyrna, admits that neither he nor anybody else could understand the wisdom of the blessed and glorious Paul.[12] The early Christian apologist Justin Martyr never mentions Paul, and Theophilus, second bishop of Antioch, refers to Paul's remarks in Romans about obedience to the state but never mentions him by name.

Ironically, the early Christian thinkers who put Paul on the map would later be condemned for heresy. Marcion, a well-educated, wealthy man who became a shipbuilder in Sinope, an important port on the Black Sea, believed that Paul had been the only apostle who had been true to Jesus's teachings. His reform movement spread so rapidly that when he died in 160, "Marcionism" was in danger of eclipsing the mainstream church. He skillfully put together a single gospel, based on the gospel of Luke and Paul's occasional letters, which he raised to the stature of scripture. His "New Testament" was founded on a rejection of the Hebrew Bible, now dismissed as the "Old Testament," which, he believed, preached a different God from the God of Jesus. The old Creator God, who had offered salvation only to the Jews and had revealed the law, Marcion argued, was violent and vengeful, whereas the God of Jesus was merciful to all and had revealed the gospel of love.

None of Marcion's works have survived; we have only fragments quoted in the writings of his opponents. It seems that Marcion probably did not dismiss the entire Torah but quoted with approval its insistence on the love of God and neighbor. But his insistence that Jesus's was a wholly new revelation meant that it was impossible to present Paul's view that Jesus was the fulfillment of Jewish history. His communities were ascetic and somewhat puritanical: they took Paul's cautious recommendation of the single life to an extreme and practiced strict celibacy; at baptism, everybody renounced the Creator God's command to "go forth and multiply"[13] and disdained the pleasures of food and drink, even to the extent of drinking water instead of wine at the Lord's Supper. But Marcion did understand Paul's egalitarianism and his concern for the poor and disenfranchised. His was the first church to follow Paul in promoting the ministry of women; in his communities, women were permitted to heal and teach and were ordained as bishops and presbyters; he also shared Paul's understanding of the link between freedom and salvation.

In order to rebut his teachings, Marcion's opponents had to study Paul more carefully. Among the earliest of these may have been the authors of the so-called Pastoral Epistles to Timothy and Titus, which were written in Paul's name probably in the early second century in either Rome or Ephesus, though they were not attributed to him until the late second century. In both style and content, they depart from Paul's own letters far more radically than the epistles to the Colossians and Ephesians. They use many words and expressions that are entirely absent from Paul's authentic letters. They never mention the Parousia, nor do they speak of living "in Christ"; for them the Greek *pistis* does not mean "loyalty" but "the Christian faith";[14] and they never call Jesus "son of God." They are called the "pastoral" letters because they give instructions to Christian leaders, who were by this time organized into a hierarchy that we do not find in Paul's letters, consisting of bishops, presbyters, and deacons.

There are signs of an anti-Marcion polemic in the Pastorals.[15] They make Paul urge Timothy to "turn a deaf ear to empty and irreligious chatter, and the antitheses which some falsely call gnosis,"[16] clearly a slighting reference to Marcion's famous treatise *Antitheses*. The same letter condemns those who "forbid marriage, and insist on abstinence from foods which God created to be enjoyed with thanksgiving by believers."[17] They clearly disapproved of Marcion's women in ministry; instead, they insisted that women should earn their salvation through childbearing and subservience: "Their role is to learn, listening quietly and with due submission. I do not permit women to teach or dictate to the men; they should keep quiet. For Adam was created first and Eve afterwards; moreover it was not Adam who was deceived, it was the woman, who, yielding to temptation, fell into sin."[18]

The Pastoral Epistles were clearly worried about false gnosis. The codices discovered at Nag Hammadi in Egypt in the 1940s revealed writings and gospels of those who sought salvation through a special, esoteric "knowledge." Gnosticism spread through Italy and the eastern provinces during the second century and, like Marcionism, was deeply troubling to those like Irenaeus, bishop of Lugdunum, who dubbed them "heretics" who departed from the teachings of the gospels and "went their own way" (*airesis* in Greek). According to the gnostic myth, which would surface also in Jewish and Islamic mysticism, a crisis within the Godhead led to the birth of the Demiurge, the creator of the lower evil world of flesh and sin. During this primal event, some divine sparks were lodged in a few men and women who formed a spiritual elite (*pneumatikoi*), but the rest, the *psychikoi*, were devoid of Spirit and insight. But they could be saved by the Christos, who descended to earth, became one with the man Jesus, and achieved the liberating knowledge (*gnosis*) of their true origin and destiny.

For Valentinus, the most influential of the second-century gnostic teachers, Paul was a major inspiration.[19] Had he not clearly defined the distinctions among "spiritual," "psychic," and fleshly "somatic" human beings in his first letter to the Corinthians? The Christ Hymn in his letter to the Philippians perfectly described the descent of the Redeemer to earth. Paul had admitted that there was no goodness in his "unspiritual" self and had cried in anguish, "Wretched creature that I am, who is there to rescue me from this state of death?" He had also proclaimed, "All things are lawful to me!," understanding that the *pneumatikoi* were free to eat meat that had been sacrificed to idols and were not bound by the pettifogging rules of the mainstream church.

This was, of course, a misinterpretation of Pauline teaching, since in his letter to the Corinthians Paul had been satirizing the beliefs of the *pneumatikoi* in Corinth, not endorsing them. But that was so often to be his fate in his afterlife. The authors of Colossians and Ephesians felt obliged to abandon Paul's egalitarianism and political stance against imperial tyranny; the Pastoral Epistles introduced a misogyny into Christianity that has been unfairly laid at Paul's door. Augustine's doctrine of original sin, based on a reading of Paul in a Latin translation, was quite alien to Paul's thought, as was Luther's signature dogma of justification by faith. Paul, who never denied his Jewishness, has been dubbed an anti-Semite. It was Marcion and the Gnostics who made Paul a prominent figure, who introduced into the Christian imagination a suspicion of Judaism and the Hebrew Bible that would have fateful consequences.

Paul has been blamed for ideas that he never preached, and some of his best insights about the spiritual life have been ignored by the churches. His passionate identification with the poor is unheeded by those Christians who preach the Prosperity Gospel. His determination to eradicate the ethnic and cultural prejudices that divide us from one another, his rejection of all forms of "boasting" based on a spurious sense of privilege and superiority, and his visceral distrust of a self-indulgent spirituality that turns faith into an ego trip have not become part of the Christian mind-set. How would Paul have reacted had he witnessed the popes stepping into the shoes of the emperors after the fall of the Roman Empire in the western provinces? There are many opinionated religious people who would do well to heed Paul's warnings to the "strong" who were intimidating the "weak" with their overbearing certainty. Above all, we need to take seriously Paul's insight that no virtue was valid unless it was imbued with a love that was not a luxurious emotion in the heart but must be expressed daily and practically in self-emptying concern for others.

Karen Armstrong is a best-selling author noted for her memoirs and her books about religion. She majored in English at St. Anne's College, Oxford, while living in a convent, an experience she wrote about in *Through the Narrow Gate,* which was published to laudatory reviews. She became an independent writer and has since published twenty-five books. In great demand as a public speaker, she is also the founder of the Charter for Compassion, which was funded with a TED grant. In 2015 she was awarded the OBE for Services to Literature and Interfaith Dialogue in Queen Elizabeth's Birthday Honours List.

Notes

Introduction

1   Matthew 27:37; unless otherwise stated, all quotations from the New Testament are taken from *The Revised English Bible* (Oxford: Oxford University Press, 1989).

2   Martin Hengel, *Crucifixion in the Ancient World and the Folly of the Message of the Cross,* trans. John Bowden (London: SCM Press; Philadelphia: Fortress Press, 1977), 76.

3   Flavius Josephus, *The Jewish War,* trans. G. A. Williamson (Harmondsworth, UK: Penguin, repr. 1967), 2:75 (hereafter cited as *JW*); Flavius Josephus, *The Antiquities of the Jews,* trans. William Whiston (Marston Gate, Amazon.co.uk. Ltd., n.d), 17:205 (hereafter cited as *AJ*).

4   *JW* 5:449–51.

5   John Dominic Crossan, *Jesus: A Revolutionary Biography* (San Francisco: Harper, 1995), 172–78.

6   1 Corinthians 15:4.

7   Richard A. Horsley, *Jesus and the Spiral of Violence: Popular Jewish Resistance in Roman Palestine* (San Francisco: Harper & Row, 1987), 286–89; Seán Freyne, *Galilee, from Alexander the Great to Hadrian, 323 BCE to 135 CE: A Study of Second Temple Judaism* (Wilmington, DE: M. Glazier; Notre Dame, IN: University of Notre Dame Press, 1980), 283–86.

8   *AJ* 19:36–38; Richard A. Horsley, "The Historical Context of Q," in Richard A. Horsley with Jonathan A. Draper, *Whoever Hears You Hears Me: Prophets, Performance, and Tradition in Q* (Harrisburg, PA: Trinity Press International, 1999), 58.

9   Matthew 3:7–10; Luke 3:7–9.

10 Isaiah 1:15–17. Unless otherwise stated, all quotations from the Hebrew Bible are taken from *The Jerusalem Bible,* ed. Alexander Jones (London: Darton, Longman & Todd, 1966).

11 *JW* 2:142–44.

12 Luke 3:11.

13 Luke 3:21–22.

14 Luke 4:14.

15 Mark 1:14–15 (my translation).

16 Matthew 9:36.

17 Warren Carter, "Construction of Violence and Identities in Matthew's Gospel," in Shelly Matthews and E. Leigh Gibson, eds., *Violence in the New Testament* (New York: T. & T. Clark, 2005), 93–94.

18 John Pairman Brown, "Techniques of Imperial Control: The Background of the Gospel Event," in Norman Gottwald, ed., *The Bible of Liberation: Political and Social Hermeneutics* (Maryknoll, NY: Orbis Books, 1983), 357–77; Warren Carter, *Matthew and the Margins: A Sociopolitical and Religious Reading* (Sheffield, UK: Sheffield Academic Press, 2000), 17–29, 36–43, 123–27, 196–98.

19 A. N. Sherwin-White, *Roman Society and Roman Law in the New Testament* (Oxford: Clarendon Press, 1963), 139; Matthew 18:22–33, 20:1–15; Luke 16:1–13; Mark 12:1–9.

20 Horsley, *Jesus and the Spiral,* 167–68.

21 A. E. Harvey, *Strenuous Commands: The Ethic of Jesus* (London: SCM Press; Philadelphia: Trinity Press International, 1990), 162, 209.

22 Luke 6:20–21; cf. vv, 24–25.

23 Luke 14:23–24.

24 Matthew 20:16.

25 Luke 6:29–31.

26 Luke 11:2–4, as translated in Stephen J. Patterson, *The Lost Way: How Two Forgotten Gospels Are Rewriting the Story of Christian Origins* (New York: HarperOne, 2014), 94.

27 Leviticus 25:23–28, 35–55; Deuteronomy 24:19–22; Norman Gottwald, *The Hebrew Bible in Its Social World and in Ours* (Atlanta, GA: Scholars Press, 1993), 162.

28 Deuteronomy 15.

29   Richard A. Horsley and Neil Asher Silberman, *The Message and the Kingdom: How Jesus and Paul Ignited a Revolution and Transformed the Ancient World* (Minneapolis, MN: Fortress Press, 1997), 56–57.

30   Luke 10:2–9; Paul was familiar with this teaching: 1 Corinthians 10:27.

31   John Dominic Crossan, *The Historical Jesus: The Life of a Mediterranean Jewish Peasant* (San Francisco: Harper, 1991), 341–44.

32   Luke 12:51–53.

33   Luke 14:27.

34   Luke 9:60, 14:26.

35   Matthew 11:18–19; Luke 7:33–34.

36   1 Corinthians 15:4–7.

37   Joel 2:28–29.

38   Psalms of Solomon 17:31–37, cited in Horsley and Silberman, *The Message and the Kingdom,* 15.

39   Horsley and Silberman, *The Message and the Kingdom,* 100–103.

40   Matthew 15:24.

41   Acts 4:32–35.

42   2 Corinthians 11:24–25.

43   Acts 11:26, 26:28 (on the lips of Herod Agrippa II); 1 Peter 4:16 (c. 100 CE).

Chapter 1: Damascus

1   Acts 2.

2   Psalm 110:1.

3   Acts 2:13–28.

4   Psalm 2:7.

5   Psalm 8:5–6.

6   Daniel 7:13–14.

7   Martin Hengel, "Christology and New Testament Chronology: A Problem in the History of Earliest Christianity" and "'Christos' in Paul," in *Between Jesus and Paul: Studies in the Earliest History of Christianity,* trans. John Bowden (Philadelphia: Fortress Press, 1983).

8   Hengel, "Between Jesus and Paul: The 'Hellenists,' the 'Seven' and Stephen (Acts 6:1–15; 7:54–8:3)," in *Between Jesus and Paul.*

9   Ibid., 28–29.

10   Luke 11:42.

11   Mark 11:17; Isaiah 56:7; Martin Hengel, *The Pre-Christian Paul*, trans. John Bowden (Philadelphia: Trinity Press International, 1991), 81–83.

12   Acts 6:1–5.

13   Acts 8:4–6.

14   Acts 6:13–14.

15   Mark 13:1–2.

16   Acts 7:56–8:1.

17   Philippians 3:5–6.

18   Hengel, *Pre-Christian Paul*, 19–60.

19   Galatians 1:14.

20   Richard A. Horsley, "Introduction," in Richard A. Horsley, ed., *Paul and Empire: Religion and Power in Roman Imperial Society* (Harrisburg, PA: Trinity Press International, 1997), 206.

21   Numbers 25.

22   Acts 2:46.

23   Acts 5:34–39.

24   1 Corinthians 1:22–25.

25   Deuteronomy 21:22–23.

26   Galatians 3:13.

27   Acts 8:3.

28   Galatians 1:13.

29   Acts 8:1; my emphasis.

30   Acts 11:19.

31   Acts 9:1–2.

32   Hengel, *Pre-Christian Paul*, 76–77.

33   Paula Fredriksen, "Judaism, the Circumcision of Gentiles, and Apocalyptic Hope: Another Look at Galatians 1 and 2," *Journal of Theological Studies* 42, no. 2 (Oct. 1991): 532–64.

34   John Knox, *Chapters in a Life of Paul*, rev. ed. (Macon, GA: Mercer University Press, 1987), 95–106; Arthur J. Dewey et al., trans., *The Authentic Letters of Paul: A New Reading of Paul's Rhetoric and Meaning* (Salem, OR: Polebridge Press, 2010), 149–150; Horsley and Silberman, *The Message and the Kingdom*, 122–26; Krister Stendahl, *Paul among Jews and Gentiles* (Philadelphia: Fortress Press, 1976); Martin Hengel and Anna Maria Schwemer, *Paul between Damascus and Antioch: The Un-*

known Years, trans. John Bowden (London: SCM Press, 1997), 39–42; Dieter Georgi, *Theocracy in Paul's Praxis and Theology,* trans. David E. Green (Minneapolis, MN: Fortress Press, 1991), 18–25.

35 Acts 9:3–6, 22:5–16, 26:10–18.

36 Romans 7:19; Robert Jewett, "Romans," in James D. G. Dunn, ed., *The Cambridge Companion to St Paul* (Cambridge, UK: Cambridge University Press, 2003), 97–98.

37 Romans 7:22–25.

38 1 Corinthians 9:1.

39 Ibid.

40 1 Corinthians 15:8 (Jerusalem Bible).

41 Galatians 1:15; cf. Isaiah 49:1, 6; Jeremiah 1:5.

42 Luke 24; Acts 1:3–11.

43 Mark 16:6, 8. The last paragraph of the gospel describing Jesus's appearances was added later in order to meld Mark's account with this later tradition.

44 Alan F. Segal, *Paul the Convert: The Apostolate and Apostasy of Saul the Pharisee* (New Haven, CT, and London: Yale University Press, 1990), 38–39.

45 2 Corinthians 12:2–4, 7.

46 Knox, *Chapters,* 101–103.

47 Louis Jacobs, *The Jewish Mystics* (London: Kyle Cathie, 1990), 23.

48 Segal, *Paul the Convert,* 39–64.

49 Ezekiel 1:26, 28; 2:1.

50 Exodus 23:20–21; my emphasis.

51 John 1:14.

52 Philippians 2:6–11.

53 Galatians 1:16.

54 Galatians 1:15–16, as translated in Segal, *Paul the Convert,* 13.

Chapter 2: Antioch

1 Galatians 1:16–17.

2 Genesis 16:3–16, 21:8–21.

3 Isaiah 60:7; Jeremiah 12:15–17.

4 Horsley and Silberman, *The Message and the Kingdom,* 124–25; Hengel and Schwemer, *Paul between Damascus and Antioch,* 109–11.

5 1 Corinthians 4:12.

6 Acts 18:3.

7 M. Aboth 2:2. It is only Luke who claims that Paul studied with Gamaliel (Acts 22:3); Paul never mentions this.

8 Cf. Galatians 6.11. For Paul as a tentmaker, see the excellent monograph of Ronald F. Hock, *The Social Context of Paul's Ministry: Tentmaking and Apostleship* (Minneapolis, MN: Fortress Press, 2007).

9 Acts 18:3, 11.

10 1 Thessalonians 2:9.

11 John Kautsky, *The Politics of Aristocratic Empires,* with a new introduction by the author (New Brunswick, NJ: Transaction Publishers, 1997), 178.

12 Thorstein Veblen, *The Theory of the Leisure Class: An Economic Study of Institutions* (Boston: Houghton Mifflin, 1973), 41, 45.

13 Philippians 2:7 (Jerusalem Bible).

14 1 Corinthians 9:19.

15 2 Corinthians 6:5.

16 1 Corinthians 4:11–13.

17 Galatians 3:6–9.

18 Galatians 4:22–24.

19 Romans 7:7, 13, 23.

20 Romans 7:14–15.

21 Genesis Apocryphon 15–19.

22 Romans 4.

23 Genesis 12:3, 15:6; cf. Romans 4:1–25.

24 Romans 3:29–31.

25 Luke 3:8Q.

26 Luke 13:28Q.

27 2 Corinthians 11:32–33; Acts 9:25.

28 Galatians 1:18, 23.

29 Acts 10:1–11:18.

30 Galatians 1:21.

31 Genesis Apocryphon 15–19; Hengel and Schwemer, *Paul between Damascus and Antioch,* 174–77.

32 Book of Jubilees 8:12.

33 Acts 11:20–21; Hengel and Schwemer, *Paul between Damascus and Antioch*, 189–91.

34 Acts 11:22–24, 13:1.

35 Segal, *Paul the Convert*, 86–87.

36 Acts 11:25–26.

37 Acts 11:26.

38 Hengel and Schwemer, *Paul between Damascus and Antioch*, 226.

39 1 Thessalonians 4:11; Romans 13:1–3.

40 Writing at the end of the first century, Clement of Alexandria (c. 150–c. 215) believed that Barnabas had been one of the seventy-two disciples of Jesus who were sent out on the mission to the Galilean villages (*Stromata* 2.20.112; Hengel and Schwemer, *Paul between Damascus and Antioch*, 218).

41 Cf. Galatians 3:28 (adapted).

42 Galatians 2:3, 7–5; Hengel and Schwemer, *Paul between Damascus and Antioch*, 292–93; Georgi, *Theocracy*, 13.

43 1 Corinthians 11:23–32; Mark 14:22–25.

44 Hengel and Schwemer, *Paul between Damascus and Antioch*, 288–90.

45 Acts 13:1.

46 Acts 13:3.

47 Hengel and Schwemer, *Paul between Damascus and Antioch*, 233–36.

48 Acts 13:4–12; cf. Exodus 7:8–12; 1 Kings 18:20–40.

49 Acts 13:12, 45.

50 Horsley and Silberman, *The Message and the Kingdom*, 130–31.

51 Ibid., 131–39.

52 Deuteronomy 17:14–15.

53 M. Sotah 7:8; my emphasis.

54 Mark 3:17; Luke 6:14. In the earliest lists of the Twelve, James appears immediately after Peter and before his brother John, so he may have been the "second man" in the group.

55 Acts 12:1–2.

56 Acts 4:6.

57 Acts 12:17.

58 Quoted in Robert Eisenman, *James, the Brother of Jesus: Recovering the*

True History of Early Christianity (London: Faber and Faber, 1997), 310.

59 Ibid., 353–54.

60 Acts 12:21–23.

61 Segal, *Paul the Convert,* 190–94, 204–23.

62 Acts 15:1.

63 Galatians 3:23–24.

64 Acts 15:2.

65 Galatians 2:2.

66 Ibid.

67 Galatians 2:4.

68 Galatians 2:7–8; my emphasis.

69 Galatians 2:9b.

70 Galatians 2:10.

71 Horsley and Silberman, *The Message and the Kingdom,* 142.

72 Georgi, *Theocracy,* 34–41.

73 Eisenman, *James, the Brother of Jesus,* 226–27.

74 Acts 15:28–29.

75 Leviticus 17:5–11.

76 Galatians 2:11–15.

77 Horsley and Silberman, *The Message and the Kingdom,* 143–44.

78 Isaiah 56:3, 7.

79 Isaiah 49:6.

Chapter 3: Land of Japheth

1 Acts 16:1–3.

2 Acts 21:21; Segal, *Paul the Convert,* 218–19.

3 Acts 16:6.

4 Galatians 4:13–14.

5 Horsley and Silberman, *The Message and the Kingdom,* 158–61.

6 Galatians 1:3–4.

7 Horsley and Silberman, *The Message and the Kingdom,* 149–52; Dewey et al., trans., *Authentic Letters of Paul,* 37.

8 Galatians 5:1.

9 Robert Jewett, "Response: Exegetical Support from Romans and Other Letters," in Richard A. Horsley, ed., *Paul and Politics: Ekklesia, Israel, Imperium, Interpretation* (Harrisburg, PA: Trinity Press International, 2000), 93.

10 Galatians 3:6–10.

11 Galatians 1:6ff.

12 Galatians 3:2–5; Knox, *Chapters,* 115.

13 Galatians 5:18.

14 Galatians 4:6–7; Horsley and Silberman, *The Message and the Kingdom,* 150.

15 Neil Elliott, "Paul and the Politics of Empire: Problems and Prospects," in Horsley, ed., *Paul and Politics,* 34.

16 Dewey et al., trans., *Authentic Letters,* 14.

17 Elliott, "Paul and the Politics of Empire," in Horsley, ed., *Paul and Politics,* 34.

18 Galatians 3:27–28.

19 Galatians 5:13–14.

20 Galatians 5:20–21.

21 Galatians 6:2–5.

22 Acts 16:6–10.

23 Dewey et al., trans., *Authentic Letters,* 165; Erik M. Heen, "Phil 2:6–11 and Resistance to Local Timocratic Rule: Isa Theo and the Cult of the Emperor in the East," in Richard A. Horsley, ed., *Paul and the Roman Imperial Order* (Harrisburg, PA: Trinity Press International, 2004), 134–35; Horsley and Silberman, *The Message and the Kingdom,* 152–54.

24 Martin P. Nilsson, *Greek Piety,* trans. Herbert J. Rose (Oxford: Clarendon Press, 1948), 178; Glen W. Bowersock, *Augustus and the Greek World* (Oxford: Clarendon Press, 1965), 112.

25 Virgil, *The Eclogues: The Georgics,* trans. C. Day Lewis (Oxford: Oxford University Press, 1999), Eclogue IV, 4–7.

26 Corpus Inscriptionum Graecorum 39576, translated in John D. Crossan and Jonathan L. Reed, *In Search of Paul: How Jesus's Apostle Opposed Rome's Empire with God's Kingdom* (San Francisco: HarperSanFrancisco, 2004), 239–40.

27 Crossan and Reed, *In Search of Paul,* 235–36.

28 S. R. F. Price, *Rituals and Power: The Roman Imperial Cult in Asia*

Minor (Cambridge and New York: Cambridge University Press, 1984); Paul Zanker, *The Power of Images in the Age of Augustus* (Ann Arbor: University of Michigan Press, 1988).

29 Price, *Rituals and Power,* 49.

30 Horsley, introduction to "The Gospel of Imperial Salvation," in Horsley, ed., *Paul and Empire,* 11–13.

31 Heen, "Phil 2:6–11," in Horsley, ed., *Paul and the Roman Imperial Order.*

32 Philippians 3:20; translation suggested by Knox, *Chapters,* 114–15.

33 Philippians 2:3–4.

34 Philippians 2:15.

35 Philippians 4:3.

36 Philippians 4:15.

37 Holland L. Hendrix, "Thessalonicans Honor Romans" (ThD thesis, Harvard Divinity School, 1984), 253, 336; Karl P. Donfried, "The Imperial Cults of Thessalonica and Political Conflict in 1 Thessalonians," in Horsley, ed., *Paul and Empire,* 217–19.

38 Hendrix, "Thessalonicans Honor Romans," 170.

39 Dewey et al., trans., *Authentic Letters,* 27; Horsley and Silberman, *The Message and the Kingdom,* 155–56.

40 1 Thessalonians, 1:9–10.

41 Cf. 2 Corinthians 8:2–4.

42 1 Thessalonians 5:12.

43 1 Thessalonians 5:14–15.

44 1 Thessalonians 2:9; Acts 17.

45 1 Thessalonians 2:2, 3:4.

46 1 Thessalonians 4:11–12.

47 1 Thessalonians 5:5, 8.

48 Acts 17:6–7.

49 Acts 17:28.

50 Andrew Wallace-Hadrill, "Patronage in Roman Society: From Republic to Empire," in Andrew Wallace-Hadrill, ed., *Patronage in Ancient Society* (London and New York: Routledge, 1989), 73.

51 Tacitus, *The Histories,* 1.4, ed. D. S. Levene; trans., W. H. Fyfe (Oxford: Oxford University Press, 2008), 4; John K. Chow, *Patronage and Power: A Study of Social Networks in Corinth* (Sheffield, UK: JSOT Press, 1992); Horsley, introduction to "Patronage, Priesthoods, and Power," in

Horsley, ed., *Paul and Empire;* Peter Garnsey and Richard Saller, "Patronal Power Relations," in Horsley, ed., *Paul and Empire;* Richard Gordon, "The Veil of Power," in Horsley, ed., *Paul and Empire.*

52 Acts 18:2–3.

53 1 Corinthians 2:4.

54 1 Corinthians 1:26–28.

55 1 Corinthians 15:24.

56 Georgi, *Theocracy,* 60–61.

57 1 Corinthians 12:22–26 (Jerusalem Bible).

58 1 Thessalonians 5:3.

59 1 Thessalonians 4:16–17.

60 1 Thessalonians 2:19, 3:13, 4:15.

61 1 Thessalonians 4:17.

62 Donfried, "Imperial Cults," in Horsley, ed., *Paul and Empire;* Helmut Koester, "Imperial Ideology and Paul's Eschatology in 1 Thessalonians," in Horsley, ed., *Paul and Empire;* Abraham Smith, "'Unmasking the Powers': Toward a Postcolonial Analysis of 1 Thessalonians," in Horsley, ed., *Paul and the Roman Imperial Order;* Georgi, *Theocracy,* 25–27.

63 Acts 18:12; not all scholars accept that Paul did coincide with Gallio.

64 Acts 18:24.

Chapter 4: Opposition

1 Horsley and Silberman, *The Message and the Kingdom,* 169–70.

2 Galatians 4:8–10.

3 Galatians 1:6, 3:1–4, 5:1–12, 6:12–13; Mark D. Nanos, *The Irony of Galatians: Paul's Letter in First-Century Context* (Minneapolis, MN: Fortress Press, 2002), 193–99; Mark D. Nanos, "Inter- and Intra-Jewish Political Context of Paul's Letter to the Galatians," in Horsley, ed., *Paul and Politics,* 146–56.

4 Galatians 5:4.

5 B. Sanhedrin 13:2; Alan F. Segal, "Response: Some Aspects of Conversion and Identity Formation in the Christian Community of Paul's Time," in Horsley, ed., *Paul and Politics,* 187–88.

6 Krister Stendhal, *Paul among the Jews and Gentiles* (Philadelphia: Fortress Press, 1976), 69–71.

7 Dewey et al., trans., *Authentic Letters,* 42–47.

8 Ibid., 159–60.

9 Galatians 3:1.

10 Galatians 2:16, 3:13.

11 Dewey et al., trans., *Authentic Letters,* 65–66; Georgi, *Theocracy,* 36.

12 Galatians 4:1–5.

13 Galatians 3:24.

14 Galatians 3:26–28.

15 Dieter Georgi, "God Turned Upside Down," in Horsley, ed., *Paul and Empire,* 159–60.

16 Georgi, *Theocracy,* 33–52.

17 Horsley and Silberman, *The Message and the Kingdom,* 171–75; Chow, *Patronage and Power;* Dewey et al., trans., *Authentic Gospel,* 73–75.

18 Acts 18:25.

19 Matthew 3:17; Luke 3:22; Patterson, *Lost Way,* 218–22.

20 Romans 1:4.

21 1 Corinthians 4:8–9.

22 1 Corinthians 3:1–4.

23 1 Corinthians 12:1, 8; 14:2, 7–9.

24 Richard A. Horsley, "Rhetoric and Empire—and 1 Corinthians," in Horsley, ed., *Paul and Politics,* 85–90.

25 Ibid., 87–89; Wisdom of Solomon 6:1, 5.

26 1 Corinthians 1:26.

27 1 Corinthians 2:13, 15.

28 1 Corinthians 16:12, 10:23.

29 1 Corinthians 8:4–6.

30 1 Corinthians 5:1–5, 6:15–17.

31 1 Corinthians 6:1–3.

32 Wisdom of Solomon 7:26–27, 29; 8:1.

33 1 Corinthians 1:20.

34 1 Corinthians 1:22–24.

35 1 Corinthians 2:7–8.

36 1 Corinthians 1:12–13.

37 1 Corinthians 6:1–3.

38 1 Corinthians 6:15.

39 1 Corinthians 5:1–7.

40 1 Corinthians 7:1–2.

41 1 Corinthians 7:10–11.

42 Elizabeth Schüssler Fiorenza, "Rhetorical Situation and Historical Reconstruction in 1 Corinthians," *New Testament Studies* 33 (1987): 386–403; Cynthia Briggs Kittredge, *Community and Authority: The Rhetoric of Obedience in the Pauline Tradition* (Harrisburg, PA: Trinity Press International, 1998).

43 1 Corinthians 7:3–4.

44 1 Corinthians 7:25–40.

45 1 Corinthians 14:33–35.

46 Kurt Aland and Barbara Aland, *The Text of the New Testament,* trans. Erroll F. Rhodes (Grand Rapids, MI: W. B. Eerdmans; Leiden: E. J. Brill, 1987), 78–81.

47 Dewey et al., trans., *Authentic Letters,* 112; Robert Jewett, "The Sexual Liberation of the Apostle Paul," *Journal of the American Academy of Religion* 47 (1979): 132.

48 1 Corinthians 11:2–16.

49 Dewey et al., trans., *Authentic Letters,* 110–11; Horsley, "Rhetoric and Empire," in Horsley, ed., *Paul and Politics,* 88.

50 1 Corinthians 11:11–12.

51 Patterson, *Lost Way,* 227–38.

52 1 Corinthians 11:21–22.

53 James 2:1–7.

54 1 Corinthians 11:27, 29.

55 1 Corinthians 2:3.

56 1 Corinthians 2:4–5, 3:20–21.

57 1 Corinthians 3:18–19.

58 1 Corinthians 8:9–11.

59 1 Corinthians 9; Stendhal, *Paul,* 60.

60 Romans 8:16, 23–26.

61 1 Corinthians 13:1.

62 1 Corinthians 14:4; Stendhal, *Paul,* 110–14.

63 1 Corinthians 15:12.

64 1 Corinthians 15:51–55.

65 1 Corinthians 15:24.

66 Dieter Georgi, *Remembering the Poor: The History of Paul's Collection for Jerusalem* (Nashville, TN: Abingdon Press, 1992), 53–54.

67 1 Corinthians 16:2.

68 Georgi, *Remembering the Poor,* 49–53.

69 Horsley and Silberman, *The Message and the Kingdom,* 176–78.

Chapter 5: The Collection

1 1 Corinthians 16:5–7.

2 2 Corinthians 1:13–22.

3 Dieter Georgi, *The Opponents of Paul in Second Corinthians: A Study of Religious Propaganda in Late Antiquity* (Edinburgh: T. & T. Clark, 1987 [1986]), 227–28, 368–89.

4 2 Corinthians 11:5, 13.

5 2 Corinthians 11:22.

6 Georgi, *Theocracy,* 62–70.

7 Plutarch, *Life of Alexander,* 329c–330d, translated in ibid., 66.

8 This letter is found in 2 Corinthians 2:14–6:13, 7:2–4. The intervening verses (6:14–7:1) are a later non-Pauline addition.

9 2 Corinthians 2:14.

10 Exodus 34:29–35.

11 2 Corinthians 3:6–17.

12 2 Corinthians 3:18.

13 2 Corinthians 4:8–10.

14 2 Corinthians 4:14, 16–18.

15 2 Corinthians 6:4–5, 9–11.

16 2 Corinthians 7:2–3.

17 2 Corinthians 10:10.

18 2 Corinthians 10–13.

19 2 Corinthians 11:16–21.

20 2 Corinthians 11:24–27.

21 2 Corinthians 11:32–33.

22 2 Corinthians 12:1–6.

23 2 Corinthians 12:7–10.

24 Acts 19:23–27.

25 2 Corinthians 1:8.

26 Philippians 1:12–30 (Jerusalem Bible).

27 Philippians 4:11.

28 Philippians 4:18.

29 Georgi, *Remembering the Poor,* 63–67.

30 2 Corinthians 2:12.

31 2 Corinthians 7:5.

32 Philippians 3:2–10. The Epistle to the Philippians is a composite document comprising perhaps three different letters that were combined by an editor, so we do not know exactly when this incident occurred.

33 2 Corinthians 1:1–2:13, 7:5–16.

34 2 Corinthians 7:7.

35 2 Corinthians 7:15.

36 2 Corinthians 7:11.

37 2 Corinthians 8:2.

38 2 Corinthians 8:7.

39 2 Corinthians 7:13; Philippians 2:2; 1 Thessalonians 3:9.

40 Georgi, *Remembering the Poor,* 71–72.

41 2 Corinthians 8:20.

42 2 Corinthians 9:1–15.

43 Isaiah 60:4–5.

44 2 Corinthians 8:13–14.

45 Romans 1:10.

46 Stendhal, *Paul,* 2.

47 Stanley K. Stowers, *A Rereading of Romans: Justice, Jews, and Gentiles* (New Haven, CT, and London: Yale University Press, 1994), 21–33.

48 Romans 1:2–5.

49 Dewey et al., trans., *Authentic Letters,* 101–102.

50 Georgi, *Theocracy,* 84.

51 Romans 1:16–17.

52 Romans 1:18–32.

53 Virgil, *Eclogues,* Georgics I, 468.

54 Horace, *Odes,* book 3, 6:45–48, translated in Stowers, *Rereading of Romans.*

55 Stowers, *Rereading of Romans,* 122–24.

56 Romans 1:29–30.

57 Georgi, *Theocracy*, 91–92.

58 Romans 2:1.

59 Romans 2:11–12.

60 Romans 3:29–30.

61 Horsley and Silberman, *The Message and the Kingdom*, 188–89; Dewey et al., trans., *Authentic Gospel*, 206–207; Georgi, *Theocracy*, 89–90.

62 Romans 3:23–27.

63 Romans 7:7–25.

64 Romans 3:20.

65 Romans 7:18–20.

66 Robert Jewett, "Romans," in James D. G. Dunn, ed., *The Cambridge Companion to St. Paul* (Cambridge and New York: Cambridge University Press, 2003), 97.

67 Romans 2:17–20.

68 Georgi, *Theocracy*, 92–93; Josiah Royce, *The Problem of Christianity* (New York: Macmillan, 1913), 107–59.

69 Genesis 3:5, 22.

70 Romans 5:7–8 (Jerusalem Bible); Dewey et al., trans., *Authentic Letters*, 208; Georgi, *Theocracy*, 96–99.

71 Romans 8:15–22.

72 Romans 8:23, 34–37.

73 Romans 13:1–7.

74 Dewey et al., trans., *Authentic Letters*, 253.

75 Horsley and Silberman, *The Message and the Kingdom*, 191.

76 Neil Elliott, "Romans 13:1–7 in the Context of Imperial Propaganda," in Horsley, ed., *Paul and Empire;* Elliott, "Paul and the Politics of Empire," in Horsley, ed., *Paul and Politics.*

77 Georgi, *Theocracy*, 102.

78 Leviticus 19:18; Romans 13:9–10.

79 Matthew 5:43–44.

80 Mark D. Nanos, *The Mystery of Romans: The Jewish Context of Paul's Letter* (Minneapolis, MN: Fortress Press, 1996), 10 passim.

81 Romans 9:2–5.

82 Romans 11:11, 25.

83 Romans 14:13–15.

84 Romans 15:26–27.

85 Scholars, however, are divided about the last chapter of Romans, which consists of a series of commendations of luminaries in the Jesus movement. Some believe that Paul was greeting members of the *ekklesia* in Rome, but others believe that this chapter was originally part of a letter to the congregation in Ephesus; it mentions Prisca and Aquila, for example, who seem to have settled in Ephesus with Paul. But others argue that after Paul's imprisonment, they might have returned to Rome.

86 Acts 20:5–6, 13–16; Georgi, *Remembering the Poor,* 123.

87 Georgi, *Remembering the Poor,* 117–18.

88 Romans 15:30–31.

89 Isaiah 60:5.

90 Isaiah 52:7; Romans 10:15.

91 Isaiah 52:1.

92 Georgi, *Remembering the Poor,* 167–68.

93 Romans 11:13–14 (Jerusalem Bible).

94 Acts 21:17–19.

95 Georgi, *Remembering the Poor,* 125–26.

96 *JW,* 2:261–62. Numbers in the ancient texts should not be taken literally.

97 Acts 21:22–25.

98 Acts 21:28.

99 Acts 28:31.

100 St. Clement, *The First Epistle to the Corinthians,* 5:6–7, translated in Andrew Louth, ed., and Maxwell Staniforth, trans., *Early Christian Writings: The Apostolic Fathers* (Harmondsworth, UK, and New York: Penguin, 1968).

101 Eusebius, *The History of the Church from Christ to Constantine,* Andrew Louth, ed., and G. A. Williamson, trans. (London and New York: Penguin, 1989), 2:25.

102 Crossan, *Jesus: A Revolutionary Biography,* 163. Crossan's emphases.

103 Ibid., 171.

Afterlife

1 Colossians 1:18.

2 Ephesians 4:15–16.

3 Colossians 1:12–13.

4 Ephesians 1:11, 21.

5 Colossians 3:18–25; cf. 1 Peter 2:18–3:7.

6 Ephesians 5:22–24.

7 James D. G. Dunn, "The Household Rules in the New Testament," in Stephen C. Barton, ed., *The Family in Theological Perspective* (Edinburgh: T. & T. Clark, 1996); David L. Balch, "Household Codes," in David E. Aune, ed., *Greco-Roman Literature and the New Testament* (Atlanta, GA: Scholars Press, 1998).

8 Ephesians 5:23–6:9.

9 1 Corinthians 15:24–27.

10 2 Peter 3:15–16.

11 Ernst Käsemann, "Paul and Early Catholicism," *New Testament Questions of Today* (Philadelphia: Fortress Press, 1969), 249; Arland J. Hultgren, "The Pastoral Epistles," in Dunn, ed., *Cambridge Companion.*

12 Polycarp, *Letters,* 3:2, in J. B. Lightfoot, ed. and trans., *The Apostolic Fathers,* 3 vols, *Part Two: S. Ignatius and S. Polycarp* (London, 1885).

13 Genesis 1:28.

14 1 Timothy 1:2; 3:9, 13; 4:6; 2 Timothy 4:7; Titus 2:2.

15 Calvin J. Roetzel, "Paul in the Second Century," in Dunn, ed., *Cambridge Companion,* 233.

16 1 Timothy 6:20.

17 1 Timothy 4:3.

18 1 Timothy 2:11–15; cf. Titus 2:3–5.

19 Elaine H. Pagels, *The Gnostic Paul: Gnostic Exegesis of the Pauline Letters* (Philadelphia: Trinity Press International, 1975), 66.